ENDORSEMENTS

"I devoured this book. Each chapter is filled with encouragement and inspiration. If you're looking for something to feed your creative soul, this is it."
—Debbie Macomber, #1 *New York Times* bestselling author

"The tenderness Mary Potter Kenyon weaves between the lines and among the very fibers of the pages of this book make it all the more a celebration and call to creativity. Inspiring. Thoughtful. A book to read, then ponder; a concept to explore, then adopt."
—Cynthia Ruchti, author of more than twenty books, including *A Fragile Hope* and *As My Parents Age*

"Mary Potter Kenyon's book is a call to explore the creative gift within all of us. It is like taking the hand of a friend who pulls us along on a new adventure, and on the way we discover new facets of ourselves. This book stirs many levels of creativity, inspiration, and blessing. It is a gift for the soul."
—Shelly Beach, speaker, consultant, author of *Love Letters from the Edge*, and winner of the Christy, Selah, Reader's Favorite, and Golden Scroll awards

"Mary Potter Kenyon has a way about her; through the written word, she has the ability to draw her reader in as if a long-time friend, sharing both light-hearted laughs and deep truths. This book is a fantastic reminder of the God-given creativity that exists within all of us and a great encouragement to take the time and effort to develop and grow in that creativity."
—Kim Harms, frequent contributor to *Today's Christian Woman* and author of the upcoming *Life Reconstructed: A Girlfriend's Guide to Mastectomy and Breast Reconstruction*

"Through her book, Mary Kenyon has stirred my thinking and bubbled up many fun childhood (and adulthood) memories. She has encouraged me to remember that our Creator God—who designed the magnificent universe, scampering squirrels, delightful tulips, and all nature that surrounds us—has uniquely and wonderfully endowed me (and each of you reading these words) with the gift of creativity. Although at times I might have downplayed the role creativity has in my life, I can see clearly now that it's ingrained in me and, when used, leads to great fulfillment. Thank you, Mary, for these important reminders and for inviting us to 'play.'"

—Twila Belk, writer, speaker, and author of *The Power to Be* and *Raindrops from Heaven*

"Remember the myth of Pandora's box? The command to keep it locked shut, for in opening it chaos will ensue? How many of us have felt the urges in us to create, but we stop, keeping the lid shut tight, fearing rejection, not believing in ourselves, thinking it's too late to start, or if we try we will look totally ridiculous? In *Called to Be Creative*, Mary Potter Kenyon gives us a fresh, friendly, faithful way of looking at the box in which we've stored our imagination and dreams. Mary invites us to lift the lid and discover the wonder, inspiration, beauty, and grace that God has placed in each of us, gifts that are released through the process of creativity. She does not do this alone, but rather weaves together stories, insights, and research from an amazing collection of other creative people in a way that inspires us to get moving, to risk, discover and enjoy the creative life, in everyday ways."

—Rev. Vicki Jolene Lindley Reece, United Methodist pastor, writer and producer of the Catholic television show *Real to Real,* recipient of Proclaim award from the Catholic Communications Campaign

"Mary Potter Kenyon understands that creativity is the soul of living. As co-creator of beauty—alongside God as Creator—Kenyon captures her own understanding of beauty and art through her heritage and in her losses. Beauty, as she knows, often emerges from the ashes of suffering and loss. Everything has the potential to become a beautiful masterpiece. Kenyon is an attentive and receptive author. In *Called to be Creative*, she makes us aware of our societal need for true beauty, and she knows deeply that each of us has the potential to create great things."

—Jeannie Ewing, author of *From Grief to Grace* and *Waiting with Purpose*

"*Called to Be Creative* is a treasure and a joy to read. Mary Potter Kenyon skillfully braids together stories about her personal life, stories about the lives of people she knows, philosophical ideas, practical advice, current research, and interesting and motivating activities for the reader, creating something that makes you want to put the book down and start creating something wonderful. My own creative life is never going to be the same having read this book, and it is also positively affecting my teaching, parenting, and way I relate to the world."

—Doug Shaw, author of *Social Nonsense: Creative Diversions for Two or More Players - Anytime, Anywhere* and professor of mathematics at the University of Northern Iowa

"*Called to Be Creative* takes the reader on a personal journey through the merry and often meandering world of creativity. As an art museum educator, I delight in the untethered creativity of the young and am dismayed when their older counterparts murmur the fateful words during art class: "Is this done right?" Mary Potter Kenyon's book reminds us that creativity is a gift that is ours to access; one is never too old or too disinclined. She provides life-affirming stories and thoughtful suggestions to ignite creativity in even the most linear thinker. I invite you to use this book as a road map as you discover for yourself the joy-filled world of self-expression."

—Margaret Buhr, Director of Education, Dubuque Museum of Art

Over the past thirty years, I've read dozens of books on creativity and enjoyed most of them. Many of the books defined and illustrated creativity. Some offered excellent tips on how to open our creative veins. A few focused on creative experiences but contained little content. *Called to be Creative* uniquely combines vast research and practical applications while avoiding the pitfall of intellectualism. The richest flavor of the book comes from Mary Potter Kenyon's shared experiences. Through reading them, we readily absorb practical ways to harness our God-given talents.

—Cecil Murphey, *New York Times* bestselling author

"With heartfelt reflection and charm, *Called to Be Creative* portrays a core foundation of creativity: Planted deeply within each of us from birth, the creative life begins in our heart, our soul, our mind, our home, and radiates from there, making the world a brighter place for everyone."

—John Schlimm, author, educator, advocate, and creator of such Participatory Art projects as THE SMILE THAT CHANGED THE WORLD (is yours)

"Every child is an artist.
The problem is how to remain
an artist once we grow up."

—PABLO PICASSO

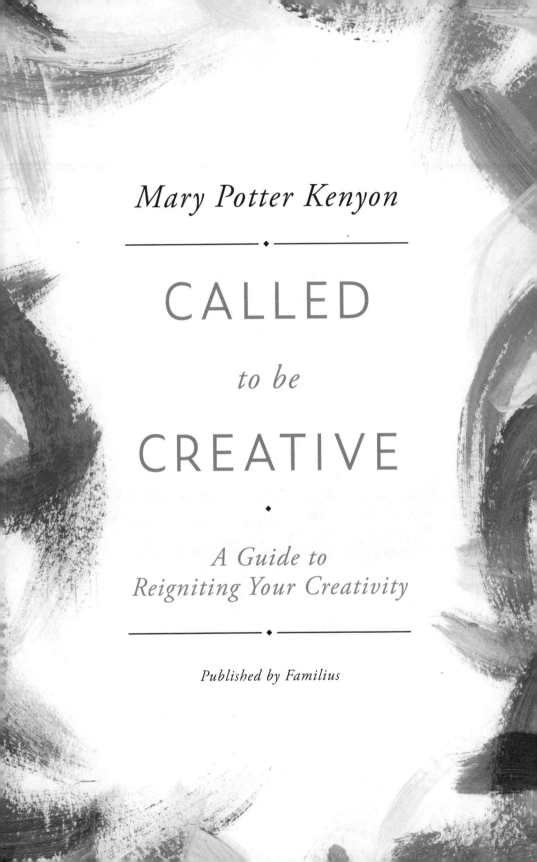

Mary Potter Kenyon

CALLED

to be

CREATIVE

*A Guide to
Reigniting Your Creativity*

Published by Familius

Published by Familius LLC, www.familius.com
1254 Commerce Way, Sanger, CA 93657

Familius books are available at special discounts for bulk purchases,
whether for sales promotions or for family or corporate use.
For more information, contact Familius Sales at 559-876-2170
or email orders@familius.com.

Library of Congress Control Number: 2020936660

Print ISBN 9781641702720
Ebook ISBN 9781641703611

Printed in the United States of America

Edited by Shaelyn Topolovec, Sarah Echard, and Peg Sandkam
Cover and book design by Mara Harris
Author photo on back cover by John Potter

10 9 8 7 6 5 4 3 2 1
First Edition

CALLED

to be

CREATIVE

A Guide to
Reigniting Your Creativity

This book is dedicated to my mother, Irma Rose "Amy" Potter, and my children: Daniel, Elizabeth, Michael, Rachel, Matthew, Emily Rose, Katherine, and Abigail

CONTENTS

FOREWORD

In our overstressed and overworked lives today, we are facing a crisis of spiritual hunger, emotional disconnection, and an abandonment of our well-being. We have placed personal fulfillment and the nourishment of our sacred inner selves on the back burner, and as a result, we find ourselves facing burnout and internal emptiness. While creativity is an elixir for so many of our problems today, many think, *I don't have a creative bone in my body; creativity is not for me.*

That creativity is reserved for artists or a select chosen few is a myth that needs immediate correction. At an all-too-critical stage in many of our lives, creativity was squashed out of us when we were told "You are not good enough" or "You have no talent." What could have become the most powerful force in our life toolboxes was extinguished through this form of Post-Traumatic Art Disorder. Yet it is never too late to nurture our spirits through creativity. There is no better time than now for us to rewrite the script of creativity's potential role in our lives.

The capacity to be creative is within us all. If you are alive, you are creative! From caveman paintings to the creation of cures for the most complex diseases, inner creativity is a channel of authentic expression through which our innermost thoughts, ideas, breakthroughs, emotions, longings, and truths are expressed into the world. When accessed, creativity guides us toward living as the best, most joyous, and authentic version of ourselves.

Years ago, as I overcame my own dark night of the soul, it became clear to me how crucial creative self-expression was in my own life. Paintbrush in hand, the canvas became a sacred, safe place that welcomed the full expression of my soul, guiding me to learn, grow, and blossom as an individual. I felt a life calling to share the uplifting power of creativity with as many people as possible. Thus, in 2004, I founded The Art Studio NY, New York City's #1-rated art school for ages 2–102. Through my work with thousands of people from every corner of the earth, I have witnessed firsthand how reconnecting with our inner creativity is a catalyst for personal transformation, increased happiness, and a deepened sense of purpose. As we navigate the twists and turns of life and its mysteries, I know this much is true: When we tap into the creative spiritual force that lives within each and every one of us, we come home to our most authentic selves and learn how to create the most important masterpiece of all—the canvas of our lives.

When Mary contacted me about my newly published book, *Release Your Creativity*, I felt a kindred spirit was reaching out her hand to join together in a collaborative creative revolution. Naturally, I was honored and thrilled to receive the invitation to write the foreword to her inspiring book.

Weathering many of life's storms with grace, dignity, and an open heart, Mary reclaimed her inborn creativity well into her adult years. Through her creative reunion, she learned how to transform life's most painful struggles into opportunities for her own healing, personal transformation, and, ultimately, the creation of a more joyful, purposeful life.

As an accomplished author, public speaker, and community leader, Mary opens the home of her soul to us and shares how creativity can transform our lives into a richer, fuller, more meaningful expression of who we are in the world. In her touching and heartwarming book, Mary acts as a wise, trusted friend who holds our hand, chapter by chapter, through the intimate and vulnerable journey toward reuniting with our creativity.

Part memoir, part inspiration, part education, Mary Potter Kenyon's *Called to Be Creative* offers a genuine and thoughtful voice that inspires the reader to reap the rewards of embarking on a creative adventure toward self-discovery.

I trust that you will enjoy and benefit from reading this book, just as I did. In it, you will discover all of the blessings inherent in leading a more creative life.

—Rebecca Schweiger, founder/owner of The Art Studio NY, www.TheArtStudioNY.com and author of *Release Your Creativity: Discover Your Inner Artist with 15 Simple Painting Projects*

Tell your story.
Shout it. Write it.
Whisper it if you have to.
But tell it.
Some won't understand it.
Some will outright reject it.
But many will
thank you for it.
And then the most
magical thing will happen.
One by one, voices will start
whispering, "Me, too."
And your tribe will gather.
And you will never
feel alone again.

—L. R. KNOST

The Artist

He who works with his hands is a laborer;
He who works with his head and with his
hands is a craftsman;
He who works with his head and his hands
and his heart is an artist.
.... Author unknown
[The Quiltie Ladies Scrapbook, 1987]

---

*O*ur main purpose on Earth is to save our soul and try to do the will of God in all things. That also means using the talents He gave us and using them for good.

The words were my mother's, written repeatedly in her notebooks and a memory book, but they would become mine in the months and years following her death in November 2010.

My mother had lived an extremely creative life, partly by necessity, more by invention. Raising ten children in abject poverty, she beautified her home with colorful rag rugs and quilts made from scraps of material. She sewed tiny denim jumpers out of her own skirts and teddy bears from cast-off woolen coats. She managed to fill twelve hungry bellies by gutting chickens, gathering eggs, canning and freezing produce, and inventing half a dozen ways to incorporate tomatoes and potatoes into recipes. Then, during her spare time, she'd draw pastel pictures, carve beautiful wooden statues, and paint on barn boards, selling many of these creations as a home business.

By the world's standards, Mom left little of material value behind. When my siblings and I divided her things, it was the remaining wood carvings, paintings, homemade teddy bears, and quilts that each of us wanted.

No one objected when I claimed the notebooks my mother had written in at night while sitting at the dining room table. Nor did they complain when I carted home four or five versions of each of her three unpublished manuscripts or idea files she'd constructed from brown paper sacks sewn together in crude scrapbook form. As the writer in the family, it seemed apt I would become the "keeper of her words."

I can admit now that I'd also coveted her dining room table, but it went to my youngest sister, Jane.

I spent a lot of time alone in my mother's empty house during the weeks following her death, sitting at that table, praying and writing. All winter, and well into the spring, I utilized the house, reveling in the unaccustomed silence. During breaks from writing, I'd pore over the remaining boxes of her possessions, searching for clues to the enigma of a mother who'd managed to spend a lifetime practicing her varied talents.

Words collided with images from a distant past as I wrote my way through that winter. I worked in a fog of grief that brought memories of my mother and me to the forefront: the two of us at parallel play, sitting on the front porch, her with art and me with words. She would paint, sew, or carve something beautiful from a piece of wood while my teenaged self wrote angst-filled poetry or short stories. Once, we were both painting in companionable silence when we heard a noise at the entrance to the porch. My father stood there, taping a hand-written sign on the window of the closed door. *Caution. Artists at work. Don't enter these premises unless you are talented*, he'd scrawled in red ink. Years later, Mom framed the torn and wrinkled sign and gave it to me. *For Mary, one of the artists on the premises. From Mom, the other one*, she'd written in pencil on the back.

I worked on many projects in my mother's house that "winter of discontent." Ten miles from home, I'd found the room of my own that Virginia Woolf had insisted every female writer needed. I managed to accomplish as much in twelve weeks writing at my mother's table as I had in the previous twelve months at home. I credited the solitude, Mom's creative spirit, and perhaps the table itself for my productivity, worrying it would all dissipate once the house sold and the table was delivered to my sister.

It didn't. If anything, immersing myself in creativity begat even more creativity. In the year following the sale of the house, I attended my first two writers' conferences, planned and implemented a writing course for homeschooled teens, and designed another course for adults. I conducted workshops at local community colleges, which resulted in a weekly column for an area newspaper. Several of my essays were accepted for anthologies, and I began doing public speaking.

"My mother never doubted for a moment that each of her children had talent," I began in one of my first speeches. I'd been asked to speak on creativity to a room full of young homeschooling moms. "Do you believe the same thing about yours?"

The women nodded, smiling with pride.

"Do you encourage your children's natural gifts and spend money on lessons or training?"

Again came the nods. I paused before asking, "But what about you? Do you ever doubt your own inherent creativity?"

Their smiles faded. Suddenly, they couldn't meet my eyes.

A few months later, I did the same presentation for a group of women at the other end of the spectrum, empty-nesters and retirees. When I asked about their talents, their replies were heartbreaking, ranging from "I don't have any talent" to "It's too late for me now."

There's a book in this somewhere, I thought then. Once home, I made notes that I filed in a folder labeled "Creativity."

Seven years and five books later, during an equally discontented winter, when I was miserable at a job that should have been perfect for me, I spent a morning reading letters my mother had written to me during the 1980s and early 1990s, letters I hadn't looked at since. Before long, I was shaking with sobs.

What was wrong? Had cumulative grief finally caught up with me? I'd lost my mother in 2010, my husband in 2012, and my grandson the following year. But as I continued to read her letters, I realized it was the unmistakable message repeated in them: *Utilize your talents. Follow God.*

Was I utilizing my talents working for a newspaper? Writing stories on agriculture and farming topics, covering legislative coffees, school board, and supervisor meetings? I was assigned the occasional human interest story, but those were few and far between. Because of my work hours, I'd lost my own morning writing time, dropped the writing classes I'd taught at community colleges, and said no to most workshops and public speaking opportunities. I'd given up those things that brought me joy in exchange for a paycheck and health insurance.

I'd been spending a lot of time with God that winter, too, asking what He wanted me to do. When a library job with fewer hours and more free mornings was advertised, I took a leap of faith and applied for it. When I was offered the position, I was nearly giddy with excitement over the idea of having some free mornings. Unsure what the topic of my next book would be, I knew I'd be writing one.

My mother's letters continued speaking to me. I dug deeper into the trunk where I kept them, unearthing some of her notebooks, the memory book, and a binder full of articles about her, along with photographs of her art. I was fascinated with the woman who went by Mrs. Byron Potter for all her magazine subscriptions, bills, and much of her business correspondence. She remained Mrs. Byron Potter until the day she died, and nearly eight years after her death I continued to get her junk mail, addressed to the wife of Byron. My father died in 1986.

Upon further reflection, it occurred to me that she'd claimed an identity separate from her husband and children in only one aspect of her life after marriage: her artwork. While her initial wall hangings and pastel drawings were signed "I. Potter" or "Irma Potter," at some point, perhaps around the time she began selling pieces, she chose an artist name. In a newspaper interview, she told the reporter she chose the name Amy because it meant "beloved," and Amy was the creative sister in her favorite book, *Little Women*. When Mrs. Byron Potter (Irma Rose) registered "Rustics by Amy" at the county courthouse, she began signing her paintings and wood carvings "Amy."

The winter reminiscing contributed to an increased restlessness within me. I wanted to embark on a creative project. The week after I changed jobs, I submitted an article to a magazine and wrote two essays for anthologies. But I yearned for something more, something bigger. Was it perhaps time to resurrect that creativity book?

On March 11, 2017, I filled my last journal with my husband's face printed on the cover. While he was still alive, I'd ordered journals personalized with photos of the two of us together and the words *Grow old along with me*. Five years out from his death, it was a relief to finally fill the last one, to not look one more time at the quote that had become a taunt. We can *invite* someone to grow old with us but cannot demand it.

I retrieved a new journal from my cupboard, one with a photo image of my mother's table on the cover. Opening it up, I discovered

I'd begun writing in it the month after she'd died but had forgotten about it. A dozen pages were filled with quotes on creativity.

I was certain then of my next project: I'd be writing about the artisan soul each of us is born with. I pulled out the file folder I'd set aside nearly seven years earlier and pored over the contents, increasingly excited about delving into a topic that had meant so much to my mother. I made copious notes in my new journal. By April, I was ready to begin work on the book proposal. I emailed the publisher of my previous books to ask if he'd be interested in seeing it upon completion. He responded in the affirmative.

That very afternoon, my sister Jane called. After a few minutes of casual conversation, her voice changed, catching a little as she got to the point of her call.

"You know we're moving soon, to a smaller house," she began.

I felt a little prickle at the back of my neck.

She hesitated before continuing, sounding near tears. "I don't know why, but I feel like I'm supposed to give you Mom's table, that it's meant to be with you. Do you want it?"

Of course, the answer was yes. It was only after I hung up that it dawned on me: not only would I be writing a book in honor of my mother's legacy of creativity—I'd be writing it *at her table.*

Mrs. Byron Potter, Mother of Ten...

Above, Mrs. Byron Potter of Earlville, Ia., says she picks up a piece of wood "and it makes me think of something." She uses chisels to create sculptures from oak, pine, walnut and Chinese elm.

Earlville woman enjoys everything from sewing to wood carving

Mrs. Bryon Potter shows her wood carvings

Necessity becomes art

Creative Spark:
CHRISTINE HUGHES

My great-aunt Christine, a woman my mother always spoke of in a reverential tone, was steeped in imagination and faith. She was the epitome of a "creative spark," an ordinary woman who managed to introduce creativity into the everyday minutiae of home life. We should all leave such a legacy.

10   Section 2   Chicago Tribune, Thursday, October 1, 1998

OBITUARIES

Christine Hughes, 88; found fulfillment in art

By Meg McSherry Breslin
TRIBUNE STAFF WRITER

Christine Hughes left her Iowa farm town for Chicago on a whim when she was 19 and never went back. A talented artist and musician, she pursued a musical career for a short while before marrying and raising a family.

It wasn't until many years later, as a senior citizen, that Mrs. Hughes finally returned to her love of art, creating oil paintings and sketches that won accolades at numerous senior citizen art fairs throughout Chicago, including a first-place award in a senior citizen contest at a Gold Coast Art Fair.

Mrs. Hughes, 88, died Tuesday of congestive heart failure in St. Joseph's Hospital in Chicago.

Her children, who had watched their mother work hard as a secretary and a beautician throughout her life, were thrilled to see her get recognition for talents she had put on hold as a working mother.

"She was just so gifted and had such creativity, not only with music but with art, and she was a real lover of nature," said her daughter, Claudia Raack.

Even from a young age, Mrs. Hughes' daughter recognized her mother's creative talent was special. At one point, she stenciled the children's footprints on the kitchen floor beneath their places at the dinner table. Even the cat had a paw stenciled on the floor near the cat dish. When her daughter wanted to make mud pies near the sidewalk, Mrs. Hughes quilted a pad for her to sit on while she worked.

"Her creativity was always going," her daughter said. "And this was a woman who worked full time and had four children. She also had an herb and flower garden and was always making homemade soup and cookies. I don't know how she did it."

After first moving to Chicago, Mrs. Hughes won a job as an organist for silent movies at the Chicago Theatre. But only weeks after winning the job, silent movies faded as sound was introduced in theaters across the country.

Mrs. Hughes then became a secretary and typist before marrying her husband, the late Thomas, in 1932. She later became a hairdresser and opened a beauty salon, which she operated out of her Rogers Park home for many years.

After her husband died in 1965, she took on secretarial work at area churches and played the organ for Sunday masses. She retired from her secretary's job at St. Benedict's Church on the city's North Side in 1976 and quickly started taking art classes and painting more regularly. Much of her work consisted of nature scenes, but she also won awards for religious images and a painting of a woman and child, her family said.

"I'm going to remember her for her faith—it was very inspirational," her daughter said, "and for her definite creative abilities. ... She was a great little lady—so tiny and so full of energy and spirit."

Besides her daughter, Mrs. Hughes is survived by three sons, Thomas, John and Tim; seven grandchildren; and three great-grandchildren.

Visitation will be held Thursday from 3 to 8:30 p.m. at the Little Sisters of the Poor retirement center, 2325 N. Lakewood Ave., Chicago. A funeral mass will be offered Friday at 10:30 a.m. in the chapel at the Little Sisters of the Poor.

"How we spend our days is, of course, how we spend our lives."

—ANNIE DILLARD

Chapter 1:
THE CREATIVITY CONUNDRUM

I suppose when at the age of #2, I first picked up a hammer and chisel and started chipping away on a stump I officially became a woodcarver. But how did I become a wood carver? And since Art comes from inside the person, where did it come from and when did it really start?

After the last of my mother's things were removed from her house, I walked slowly through the rooms, checking for missed items, dusting every bare surface. My three youngest daughters trailed behind me. The inventory check and last-minute cleaning also served as a delay to saying goodbye to the home I'd grown up in. The house had become a refuge for me in the previous months while I'd treated it as a private writing retreat. It was hard to let it go. It was the final day before we'd close the house for good and turn the keys over to a realtor.

Running my dust cloth along the windowpanes of the front porch that had served as Mom's workroom, I contemplated all the hours she'd spent in there. My fingertips hit an object that gave a little, sliding across the sill of one window. It was an extremely thin pencil emblazoned with advertising. I held it aloft for my daughters to see.

"Look. One of Grandma's magic pencils," I teased. "Just think. This is a pencil she probably used to draw rough sketches for what would later become a painting."

The girls were well aware of Grandma's talent, impressed by her wood carvings, her barn board and canvas paintings, and the quilts and teddy bears she'd crafted. They considered her a bona fide artist. Their mother? Not so much. Scribbling down words hardly seemed a creative endeavor in comparison to painting, drawing, or wood carving. They'd never even seen the thin folder I kept hidden away in a cabinet: quirky sketches and pastel creations I'd saved from the art classes I'd loved as a teen. I'd always been enticed by creativity in its many forms, skipping the more useful home economics classes for art, drama, and creative writing.

That afternoon, I sat at my kitchen table, my mother's pencil in hand, a sheet of plain white printer paper in front of me. *I used to enjoy art classes*, I thought wistfully, wondering if I'd retained any artistic ability. As a teen, I'd labored over sketches depicting the bare bones of winter trees, with looming trunks and spindly branches, never quite having mastered the leaves. My art teacher had praised those drawings.

I began sketching, pleased to see a tree taking form on the paper. I hadn't noticed eleven-year-old Katie approach. I looked up when I heard a gasp, my eyes meeting Katie's incredulous pair. I smiled at her apparent shock, holding up the pencil with a flourish.

"You drew that?" she asked. "You can't draw. It really is a magic pencil. Can I try it next?"

Later that day, I brought out the folder, introducing my daughters to a mother they didn't know existed, the one who'd practiced art. Determined to impart a lesson, I explained that even if we have a natural talent for something, if we don't hone it with hours of work, our talents can become rusty with disuse.

"I used to enjoy sketching," I continued. "My drawing skills are as rusty as if I was a beginning art student. But I've been practicing writing for years."

Their eyes betrayed their confusion, as if wondering why anyone would choose writing over real art. That afternoon encounter led me to wonder why so many of us abandon interests we were drawn to as children. Do we each have a creative bent, some talent that could be utilized in some manner, if we practiced it? Could I have just as easily become an artist as a writer?

In the weeks and months following my mother's death, I read my way through her notebooks and the memory book she'd filled, clearly seeing instances when she'd pondered those very questions.

Science has asked the same thing, with researchers attempting to quantify and qualify the elusive concept of creativity. What makes one person more creative than another, and what about those who are considered geniuses in innovation or art? What do they possess that the rest of us don't? As an independent topic of study, creativity received no real attention until the nineteenth century. But since the 1950s, there has been a dramatic rise in research on the topic. According to "Trends in the Creativity Literature," a 1993 article in the *Creativity Research Journal*, there were more than 9,000 scientific papers published on the subject between the late 1960s and early 1990s. In the ten-year period that followed, another 10,000 were written. The fact that a journal focused entirely on the subject even exists demonstrates how creativity has become a significant topic of interest, not only for the scientific community but for the general population as well.

In their book *Wired to Create*, Scott Barry Kaufman and Carolyn Gregoire study the latest findings of neuroscience and psychology and the practices of well-known "creatives," concluding that we are all, in some way, wired for creating and that everyday life presents endless opportunities to express it.

"Creativity is not a blessing some special few are born with or receive from above," clinical psychologist Ellen J. Langer writes in her book *On Becoming an Artist*. "Our creative nature is an integral part of our daily lives, expressed through our culture, our language, and even our most mundane activities."

Dr. Gene D. Cohen, a pioneer in research on mental health and aging and the founder and first director of the Center on Aging, Health and Humanities at The George Washington University, was convinced we are built for creativity.

"Creativity is built into our species, innate to every one of us, whether we are plumbers, professors, short-order cooks, or investment bankers. It is ours whether we are career-oriented or home-centered. It is the flame that heats the human spirit and kindles our desire for inner growth and self-expression," he wrote in *The Creative Age: Awakening Human Potential in the Second Half of Life*. "Our creativity may emerge in many different ways, from the realm of art, science, or politics, to the pursuit of an advanced college degree, a new hobby, or public-spirited activism."

Though her certainty stems from a deep faith rather than neuroscience, author Jen Hatmaker is in agreement.

"I sincerely believe we are created by a Creator to be creative," she says in *Of Mess and Moxie*. "This is part of His image we bear, this bringing forth of beauty, life, newness. This bears out in one thousand different ways: we write, sculpt, paint, speak, dance, craft, film, design, photograph, draw, bring order, beautify, garden, innovate, produce, cook, invent, fashion, sing, compose, imagine. It looks like art, it looks like music, it looks like community, it looks like splendor. The thing in you that wants to make something beautiful? It is holy."

As a new wife in the early 1980s, I treated Edith Schaeffer's *The Hidden Art of Homemaking* as my handbook of housewifery. Cofounder of L'Abri, a community that hosted people "seeking intellectually honest and culturally informed answers to questions about God and the meaning of life," Schaeffer believed that a creative God who designed us in His own image would naturally endow each of us with the ability to create.

"I would define 'hidden art' as the art found in the ordinary areas of everyday life. Each person has, I believe, some talent which is unfulfilled in some hidden area of his being—a talent which could be expressed and developed," she wrote.

I took her words seriously, reveling in simple household tasks, intent on becoming a happy little homemaker. I'd set our table with colorful thrift-store cloth napkins next to the simple melamine plates we'd received as a wedding gift. I'd decorate the edges of my notebook paper with intricate flowers when I wrote letters to my parents or snail-mail friends I netted from the pen pal ads in women's magazines on grocery store stands. I'd lug baskets of laundry to the communal backyard of our married student housing complex and carefully smooth out towels as I clipped them to the clothesline. I enjoyed that last domestic chore so much, I'd immediately go back inside to search for something else I could run through the washing machine. I'd remove pillowcases and take down curtains just to have more laundry to hang. It wasn't long before cloth diapers joined the towels outside. Sometimes I'd just stand there, gazing at them whipping in the wind, noting with satisfaction how white and soft they were when I brought them in at the end of the day. The fact that I had the time to watch my laundry dry, or search for pen pals in women's magazines, says something about the slower pace and accompanying mindfulness of early motherhood with a single child during that era.

When did I lose that natural sense of accomplishment that came with everyday tasks? Was it upon the birth of baby number two, three, or four? Or did I retain it even through my sixth pregnancy, when I bleached everything in sight, washing my cotton nightgown so frequently that the bright bluebell pattern faded to a dull gray? To this day, I can recall the fresh scent of the bleached and sun-dried gown and bedsheets. It wasn't until I'd gotten through a difficult labor and delivery, and my head hit the hospital pillow, that I realized I'd attempted to replicate the smell of hospital linens—the one place I was able to get some rest. By then, I'd added homeschooling and a home business to already busy days.

Still, while I'd lost some delight with mundane chores, there was one creative endeavor I practiced with a fervor that bordered on desperation: writing. I'd get up at 5:30 a.m. (and, if my husband was home, sneak out of the house to a local restaurant for coffee) and immediately begin scribbling at a frantic pace. My first book was born the same year as my sixth child. Much like my mother before me, I'd immersed myself in a style of mothering that consumed much of my time and energy, but I was determined not to lose my creative self in the process.

I'd discovered the burning desire to write, and nothing would stop me from it. Could it just as easily have been painting or drawing? My somewhat successful attempt to draw with my mother's pencil suggested the skill could have been honed. Creativity begins with a foundation of knowledge, learning a discipline, and then mastering a skill. And, if creativity is a skill, then it's a practice that can be developed.

Businesses that depend on creative innovation learned this a long time ago. As far back as 1956, Louis R. Mobley realized it was more important for IBM's executives to think creatively than to be able to read financial reports. According to his mentee August Turak, in a 2011 *Forbes* article, the IBM Executive School was built around six principles that can be applied to everyday life.

1. Traditional teaching methods of lecturing, testing, and memorizing are counterproductive.

2. Becoming creative is an unlearning process, not learning. You need to abandon, discard, destroy, and trash beloved assumptions.

3. You don't learn to become creative. You become a creative person behaviorally, through your actions, transforming yourself. You become a creative person through practice.

4. The fastest way to become creative is to hang around with creative people. Creativity is infectious.

5. Creativity is highly correlated with self-knowledge. If you don't know what your own inner biases are, you cannot overcome them.

6. Creative people give themselves permission to be wrong, and to fail. Fail fast to succeed early, is the principle.

Preschoolers don't need to be taught to be creative. Ask any parent. Imaginative pretend play and elaborate storytelling comes naturally to youngsters. Turn them loose with a bin of craft materials and some glitter and watch what happens. There was never enough paper around to satisfy my budding artists. I'd purchase it by the case, something my mother couldn't afford to do. Despite poverty, my siblings and I still managed to find something to color on, usually flattened brown paper sacks or newsprint. Sticks would become swords, rocks built into ovens to bake our mud pies. In observing preschoolers, even poverty-stricken ones, it's easy to believe creativity is something we're born with.

Allowing then for the possibility that each of us carries within us a potential for creativity, what can happen if we actively pursue and cultivate those interests we naturally gravitated toward as children?

To cultivate our creative self means revisiting our childhood. In his book *Ignore Everybody: And 39 Other Keys to Creativity*, author

Hugh MacLeod has this to say: "Everyone is born creative; everyone is given a box of crayons in kindergarten. Then when you hit puberty they take the crayons away and replace them with dry, uninspiring books on algebra, history, etc. Being suddenly hit years later with the 'creative bug' is just a wee voice telling you, 'I'd like my crayons back, please.'"

This book is for the adult who had their crayons snatched away a long time ago and now wants them back. Those who were too busy raising families or working two jobs to make ends meet to concentrate on fanning the flame from the spark within.

"How often have we neglected activities like art, music, writing, dance—or a host of other creative endeavors—as we pursue careers and families?" Ellen J. Langer laments in *On Becoming an Artist*. "We might regretfully add them to the list of things we'll get to later, but we think little about why we are doing so. Then one day we realize that now is yesterday's later. We typically regard such creative pursuits as 'leisure' activities, and that word suggests they are rather unimportant. They may well, however, hold the key to the problem of finding meaning and fulfillment in the rest of our lives."

Wherever you fall on the spectrum—still raising children or retired—it's never too late to find meaning and fulfillment in your life. This book is geared toward the individual who is searching for an elusive something more, restless with a deep inner longing tied to finding your true purpose.

The same God that created mountain, stream, and desert beauty, who dotted a night sky with a million points of light, endowed each of us with unique gifts, a calling of sorts. I love the New Living Translation (NLT) of Ephesians 2:10: "We are God's masterpiece. He has created us anew in Christ Jesus, so we can do the good things he planned for us long ago."

Whether it means producing a piece of art, writing a short story, or simply bringing beauty into our home or into the lives of others, consider for a moment that we each have the capacity to be creative. The masterpiece, then, is not something we create to hang on our

wall but something in ourselves as we fulfill our God-given potential, utilizing the talents He gave us.

Are you ready to reclaim your box of crayons, to reinvent a
mundane life to become the masterpiece God intended? At the very
least, would you like to unleash some of your natural creativity in
your everyday life? Then you've come to the right place.

Sometimes all it takes is a magic pencil to connect to that creative child we once were, open our mind to our creative potential,
and learn to play again.

IGNITE

What did you enjoy doing as a child? What kinds of activities were you drawn to? Was it digging in the dirt? Helping Mom in the kitchen? Reading or drawing? Think back to the deep recesses of your mind.

_____

_____

_____

_____

_____

_____

_____

Were there interests or hobbies you wanted to pursue but were unable to, for whatever reason?

_____

_____

_____

_____

_____

_____

_____

What talents did parents, teachers, or other trusted adults observe in you or say you had a natural gift for?

_____

_____

_____

_____

_____

_____

_____

When you were old enough to choose for yourself, what activities, clubs, organizations, and groups did you join?

_____

_____

_____

_____

_____

_____

_____

_____

_____

Creative Spark:
CATHY CORKERY

"Not everyone wants to do arts and crafts," Cathy Corkery says, "but everyone wants to feel healthy and happy."

Ten years ago, Cathy was neither. Dealing with chronic pain, she was deeply depressed with the unrelenting discomfort. She'd hit rock bottom, briefly contemplating suicide at one point.

It hadn't always been that way. After she graduated from high school, Cathy attended Iowa State University for a year before getting married and giving birth to three children. She was kept busy managing motherhood and teaching Kindermusik and piano lessons, a home business that allowed her children to come in with their sitter for a quiet hug now and then.

Teaching private music lessons had been a lifelong dream, ever since her band director in eighth grade had arranged for her to give clarinet lessons to a girl from a neighboring farm.

"She showed up at my home on a horse," Cathy says with a laugh. "So I can say my first music student arrived on horseback."

In 1989, she purchased a piano lab and five digital pianos and began teaching group piano classes. In 1992, she took training to become a Kindermusik teacher. Her training took her to Oklahoma State, Chicago Northwestern, and Minneapolis. She was only the seventh person in Iowa to teach Kindermusik. Contrary to the fears of the company's president, the small town of Manchester, Iowa, embraced the early childhood music program.

Then chronic pain began in 2003, bringing its own set of challenges to Cathy's home business and productivity. For eight years Cathy suffered.

"It was challenging to keep the business going. I was encouraged to file for disability, but it felt better for me to keep teaching than not," Cathy says about that time. "I did hire a cleaning person as that was hard to keep up with and created more pain."

Cathy began attending yoga classes, eventually training to become a yoga instructor. In 2012, she traveled to Toronto for a Yoga Therapy Intensive course.

"I took the training to help others, not realizing it would help me," Cathy says. "Three months later, implementing these new practices, I was off all medications. Yoga therapy, meditation practice, and breath work literally saved my life."

Yoga has done more than give Cathy a new lease on life; it brought new dimensions to an already thriving home business. The breath, movement, and stillness that saved her are key elements in the yoga classes Cathy now teaches in her home studio. She's also planned and coordinated women's retreat weekends, incorporating a journal-making activity she later conducted as a workshop at a grief retreat weekend.

"Looking back now, I see that I have been a lifelong learner, making it a priority to attend professional development conferences," Cathy says. "I still do, learning new techniques, and attending yoga conferences as well. Yoga has offered me chances to travel and study in Mexico, Seattle, Denver, Toronto, Boston, Los Angeles, Iceland, and now Duluth."

Cathy is currently enrolled at SomaYoga International in Duluth, studying a yoga therapy program that blends yoga and somatics.

"It works on healing physically, emotionally, and spiritually," Cathy says. "I don't think complete healing can happen unless we include the spirit in the journey. I feel so grateful that I can offer people a treatment plan that includes their spiritual health as well."

While Cathy continues to conduct traditional hatha yoga classes, her specialty is therapeutic yoga, helping people get out of, and stay out of, pain, both physical and emotional. Outside of her scheduled classes, she holds private individual yoga sessions. She has helped cancer patients, nursing home residents, and troubled children find healing and comfort through yoga practice.

"For people dealing with pain or heartache, we are dealing with little broken pieces," Cathy says. "Yoga can help them feel whole."

Chapter 2:
THE PURSUIT OF HAPPINESS

May you live all the days of your life to see God in everything – makes life a great adventure.

One of the first projects I undertook in my position as a Senior Services librarian was to form a group I inelegantly dubbed the "Lifelong Learners Creativity Group." Forming the group made sense for a librarian. A 2015 Pew Research study revealed that adults who use libraries are more likely to consider themselves to be lifelong learners, actively pursuing learning opportunities. The International Federation of Library Associations and Institutions (IFLA) has added "lifelong learning" to the list of services all libraries should provide.

The group was consistent with a library's mission to engage learners and inspire thinkers, but the formation of it was not simply a job-related, altruistic move. It had been months since I'd felt the kind of creative energy that tended to reveal itself in the writing classes I'd conducted. I'd seen what could happen in a room full of people who invested in their craft, and I missed those passionate conversations about writing. I'd experienced the same thing at writers' conferences too; the rush of adrenaline that came with speaking and practicing one's passion, the camaraderie of being in a room full of people that shared that passion. I needed what this group could offer. It turned out others did too.

Women in the fledgling group admitted they weren't sure what they'd gain from membership, but something in the description had appealed to a restless stirring within them:

Perhaps you were the daydreamer in grade school, the child staring out the window with a head full of stories, or the one reading books from your lap beneath the desk. Then someone snatched the box of crayons from your hand, insisting you'd done it all wrong; that trees weren't pink, and bunnies weren't purple, and you'd gone outside the lines. Or maybe they pulled the book out from beneath your desk, telling you it was time for math, not reading. Whether you're ready to reignite your childhood passion for all things creative and want your crayons back, or are looking for a way to connect with your inner artist and others who think outside of the box, a new group forming at the James Kennedy Library might be of interest.

The group was not closed to males, nor was there any age restriction, yet our initial membership consisted of women ranging from their early thirties to mid-seventies. As we took turns introducing ourselves, it soon became apparent we all had one thing in common: we wanted to add creativity into our lives in some way, and we expected that doing so would make us happier.

We were correct in that assumption. Thanks to scientific research, we can be sure of one thing: working creative endeavors into our lives leads to a more positive state of mind. When researchers at the University of Otago constructed a study to understand if creativity impacted emotional well-being, they discovered a positive connection between the two. The activities could be as simple as journaling, playing an instrument, or spring gardening, as long as it had meaning for the individual.

Writing for a newspaper should have been the perfect job for me. Sitting in an office every weekday morning, I was being paid to do what I loved: write. For nearly thirty years, I'd been utilizing morning hours for writing, rising from bed before my children and scribbling away, seeing very little monetary gain. With the newspaper job, I was guaranteed an hourly wage for the same practice.

Initially, there was that sense of satisfaction from a job well done. I was adept at unearthing stories behind the stories, well qualified for the straight reporting. Within weeks, however, the novelty wore off. The constant deadlines ate away at me. There were Mondays when I attended both afternoon and evening meetings and I'd be working from 8:30 a.m. until nearly midnight to meet the Tuesday morning deadline. While with my own writing, I could spend two or three weeks working on a piece, the human interest stories that held the most meaning for me had to be written in two or three days. Then there were so few of those stories compared to meeting coverage and assignments on topics I found mind numbing.

Months into the job, my jaw ached from unconsciously clenching it and my eyelid continually twitched. Not only that, but because of time constraints, I'd given up most of the workshops and speaking opportunities I'd enjoyed. I was increasingly miserable.

The catalyst for change came the day our town experienced extensive flooding. My boss arrived at our Manchester office, primed for action, repeatedly rushing out the door to get pictures as the water savagely advanced. She was a ball of energy, her muscles taut with the possibility of an award-quality photo. She discovered it on the edge of a park, as a mother deer gently led her fawn, neck deep in the water, to the safety of the grass.

"No deer were harmed in this photo op," she joked good-naturedly as she passed the camera around our office to share the picture. Her cheeks were flushed, her eyes alight with excitement. I realized it had been months since I'd seen that same light in my own eyes.

The next morning, I was assigned to take photos depicting the aftereffects of the flood. I drove slowly through town only to discover most of the cleanup had already been accomplished. My heart sank when I reached the small mom-and-pop produce business on the edge of the flood zone. I'd interviewed the owners several times, most recently after the husband had gone through grueling cancer treatment. I'd hoped they'd escaped the devastation of the flood waters, but evidently not. The doors of their building were wide open, an oversize dumpster in back filled to the brim. I was afraid to stop there, to see the look on their faces. I truly cared about these people. But I needed a photo, and there it was, the perfect example of the aftereffects of the flooding.

The building was empty when I entered, an industrial-size fan set up to dry the drenched floors. I halfheartedly took a few pictures as I stood in the middle of the room, thinking about the last time I'd talked to the older couple. The husband had stood stoically at his wife's side as she related the treatment he'd endured, her eyes filling with tears as she spoke. I considered all they'd endured the past few years: repeated flooding of their business, cancer, and now additional flood damage.

I began sobbing then, unable to stem the flow of tears as I stumbled to my vehicle. I cried all the way home, realizing I wasn't crying just for the couple but about myself. I didn't want to be this person—someone who would take pictures of another person's misery. It was clear I needed to find a different job. It would be months before I found employment as a librarian, a position that meant fewer hours, more open mornings, and evenings available for teaching and public speaking.

Sometimes we instinctively know what will bring us happiness. I knew I'd savor the free time for writing. What surprised me was a year after the job change, I'd still be waking up excited with the freedom to write on my days off, greedy for open mornings.

I begin free mornings with nothing more than a mug of coffee, legal pad, and pen, refilling my cup several times, blissfully unaware of the passage of time as I write. Then I'll glance at the clock and realize it's the afternoon and I'm still in my pajamas. A similar thing happens when I'm teaching or speaking on subjects I'm passionate about (minus the pajamas, of course). I can hardly believe I'm getting paid to do something I enjoy so much. I've left a class on such a high I barely remember the drive home. That feeling can last for hours, even days.

Researchers call this joyful state "flow," the loss of self-consciousness that happens when we're completely absorbed in an activity, whether it's intellectual, professional, or physical. Flow can be achieved through activities such as running a race, playing the violin, or writing a book, as long as the activity is voluntary, intrinsically motivating, requiring skill, and challenging in some way.

"When we are in flow, we lose track of time and self while controlling our attention to meet challenging goals," is how Dr. Gary Gute, University of Northern Iowa professor, describes it. "We do our best and feel our best. Flow gives our intellectual and emotional resources a workout, helps us extract meaning and enjoyment from life, and powers the transformation of anxiety, boredom, and suffering."

A growing body of scientific research proves that flow is positively correlated with happiness and that people who experience a lot of flow also develop increased concentration, better performance, and higher self-esteem.

"The best moments in our lives are not the passive, receptive, relaxing times. . . . The best moments usually occur if a person's body or mind is stretched to its limits in a voluntary effort to accomplish something difficult and worthwhile," Mihaly Csikszentmihalyi claims in his book *Flow: The Psychology of Optimal Experience.*

Csikszentmihalyi is one of the pioneers of the scientific study of happiness and a founding figure of positive psychology. He discovered that people find genuine satisfaction during the flow state of consciousness, particularly with activities that involve their creative abilities. He insists happiness does not simply happen but must be prepared for and cultivated by each person by setting challenges that are neither too simple nor too demanding for one's abilities.

The main thesis of his work is that happiness is not a fixed state but one that can be developed as we learn to achieve flow in our lives. His definition of flow is "a state in which people are so involved in an activity that nothing else seems to matter; the experience is so enjoyable that people will continue to do it even at great cost, for the sheer sake of doing it."

One key aspect of flow is that while in it, nearly all the brain's available inputs are devoted to one activity, which is why the perception of time changes. The brain is too focused on one thing to keep track of stray negative thoughts, or even discomfort. That explains why a runner might experience a "runner's high," or why I can forget to eat lunch when immersed in a writing project.

While Csikszentmihalyi is quick to point out that one can achieve this state through activities such as fishing, playing the guitar, cooking, or reading, he considers the practice of hatha yoga, in particular, one of the best models to describe what happens when psychic energy is flowing.

"The similarities between yoga and flow are extremely strong; in fact, it makes sense to think of yoga as a very thoroughly planned flow activity. Both try to achieve a joyous, self-forgetful involvement through concentration, which in turn is made possible by a discipline of the body," he writes in his book.

Does that mean everyone should practice yoga? A yoga instructor might concur, but there are many other ways to establish the flow state, and it could take some experimentation to discover what works for you. I find it in writing and public speaking, but I'm open to experiencing it through other avenues, which explains one of the tenets of the lifelong learner group I facilitated at the library: to try new things. One month, a member brought ukuleles for everyone, insisting we'd be playing a tune by the end of the evening. The following month, we painted on canvas. I enjoyed both these activities, not because I had plans to become a musician or a painter but because I wanted to stretch my creative muscles. Being able to laugh good-naturedly at my clumsy attempts didn't hurt either.

Attempting something new isn't the only way to generate art's benefits. According to a study by Professor Semir Zeki, a neurobiologist at University College, London, even the simple act of *admiring* good artwork triggers a rise in dopamine, affecting the feel-good area of the brain, increasing blood flow and causing contentment.

So what are you waiting for? Want to add joy to your life? It's time to look at activities that can bring you to a state of flow.

"Fill your paper with the breathings of your heart," poet William Wordsworth *wrote.*

When was the last time you got lost in an activity? Perhaps it's just a matter of finding something you can get lost in. List all those creative endeavors you could imagine doing if lack of time or money were not a hindrance. Don't overthink this exercise or hold back because some endeavors seem impossible. Jot down the first things you think of.

_____

_____

_____

_____

_____

_____

_____

_____

_____

_____

_____

_____

_____

_____

_____

Creative Spark:
BRUNA MELO

I met Bruna Melo and her husband Ryan Howard at a writing course I taught for a community college in Cedar Falls, where they live. I sensed two things regarding the young couple that evening: Bruna had a story to tell, and they were both poised for greatness.

It would be two more years before I heard Bruna's testimony of healing and realize she was meant to be a part of the annual grief retreat I coordinated. She readily agreed to sing at the opening of the 2017 event.

Bruna began singing at parties and events when she was just three years old. By the time she was seven, her parents had placed her in music and acting classes for children. She soon moved up to singing classes, and the love for music has never left her. In 1998, at the age of fifteen, following participation in a music festival where she received first place and an award for best performance, she released her first CD. Bruna became a successful gospel singer in her native Rio de Janeiro, Brazil, where she released several CDs and was featured on Brazilian radio and television programs. She graduated with a degree in marketing, finishing her MBA in 2011. Multitalented Bruna has experience in songwriting, scriptwriting, television program hosting, modeling, acting, marketing management, fashion design, event planning, workshop facilitation, and entrepreneurship. Her most recent CD included the Portuguese version of the song "The Climb," authorized by Disney Records and Hollywood Records.

Bruna met Ryan in January 2012 while he was visiting Brazil for his work in supply management with John Deere. In January 2014, during a trip to the United States to visit the man she was slated to marry, Bruna suffered a horrible sledding accident that left her with serious injuries.

"I had to stay immobilized in bed," Bruna recalls. "It was right before the release of my new CD, and all the tour events had to be canceled. My mom took care of me, and I felt like a burden because I couldn't do simple things like go to the restroom, shower, or cook without her help. I know it was not easy for her either. I even had to learn how to walk again. Yet my mom, Ryan, and people from church were praying for me, believing that God could do a miracle in my life."

It's difficult for Bruna to talk about this period in her life when she was in agonizing pain and felt so hopeless.

"I thought everything was lost to me," Bruna continues. "That I wouldn't be able to get married or have a normal life. I was desperate with the hopeless prognosis from different doctors who told me I was destined for a life filled with pain. I became deeply depressed, asking God to take me home because I didn't want to live anymore."

Then she smiles.

"But God doesn't answer foolish prayers. If my foolish prayer had been answered, I would not be here to tell my story, sharing that we can fully trust in God because He is the master of healing and He can change something bad into good like Romans 8:28 says in the Bible. I believed what I read in the Bible about Jesus healing people with all kind of diseases, and how God can restore health completely no matter the circumstances.

"He healed me. I am living proof that only God has the last word in any situation. He not only healed me physically but also shaped me into a new Bruna, enjoying life with more simplicity, love, gratitude, and compassion," Bruna adds. "And I don't miss the old Bruna that I was before the sledding accident."

In August 2015, Bruna moved to the United States to marry Ryan. She continues singing and sharing her testimony to encourage others with a message of hope that points to God. Currently, she is working on her first English CD, along with a music video entitled "Renewal." She's working on a web TV program that shares uplifting messages, "Enjoy Every Day," on her website, BrunaMelo. com. Her husband, Ryan, continues to work at John Deere and is the founder of YourFaithAtWork.org.

"Most of us go to our grave with our music still inside us."

—OLIVER WENDELL HOLMES

Chapter 3:
THE ART OF HEALING

Our talents are on loan from God. Will we use them? The choice is ours. The answer is a personal one and our intentions are eternal in their consequences.

In her lovely book *Release Your Creativity*, renowned artist and art studio owner Rebecca Schweiger relates how certain plants and tree seeds only germinate in the heat of a raging forest fire. Without those high temperatures, the seeds would remain encased in their pods. It's the chemicals from the charred wood that nurture the growth of native plants and flowers, some of which lie dormant for years, even centuries, awakened only by the fire. Those beautiful blossoms appear only in the aftermath of massive flames.

"Chaos is a powerful catalyst for inspired change, reevaluation, and, ultimately, the creation of a deeper and more conscious, meaningful life," Schweiger writes.

That concept certainly held true for me—grieving my mother served as a catalyst for change in my creative life, the words "utilize your talents" becoming a mantra of sorts. The winter after Mom's death, I embarked on what would become one of the most creative periods of my life up to that point. In her empty house, I found solitude and solace, a private writing retreat. There, I planned a presentation for young homeschooling mothers, perfected a book proposal, and worked on a book about the obsession of extreme couponing.

The following summer, I signed up for my first writer's conference. I'd been writing for over twenty-five years, but thanks to my mother's influence and the encouragement of my husband, David, I made the decision to invest both time and money into the craft. It could be said that grief was the impetus to taking my writing seriously, the legacy of a creative mother my muse.

My supportive husband became the wind beneath my wings as I flourished physically, mentally, and emotionally. David would offer to watch the kids for an afternoon, make me a mug of hot tea, and shoo me out the door to my mother's house. He'd drive me to my workshops, claiming the time alone with me in the car was well worth the wait while I conducted them. Later, he'd tell me how much he enjoyed watching me in action.

"You're soaring," he'd say. "I love seeing you this way, following your passions. This is your time to fly."

There seemed to be no end to what I could accomplish with my newly acquired determination to utilize my God-given talents. By early 2012, I'd obtained a literary agent, was seeking publication for my completed manuscript, had designed several writing and couponing PowerPoint workshops, and had established myself as a local couponing expert through a weekly Coupon Queen newspaper column with a tri-state newspaper.

When David died that March, it would have been easy to give up the creative endeavors he'd supported and encouraged. Without him at my side, much of it seemed meaningless. Then I reminded myself how much David believed in me, how he'd reveled in my successes. How could I give up on a book that had been his idea in the first place? The workshops he'd encouraged? I was determined to continue those creative endeavors in his honor. My writing took on a frantic pace, born out of pain. I journaled, wrote essays and articles, and began work on another book. A corner of my couch turned into a paper nest, where I'd sit for hours, surrounded by piles of papers and books.

"The creative process is far too often inspired by our most painful experiences rather than our most inspiring ones. It would not be a stretch to say that for many artists, authenticity and tragedy are inseparable," Erwin Raphael McManus wrote in *The Artisan Soul: Crafting Your Life into a Work of Art*.

Interest in how trauma can be a catalyst for positive change took hold in the mid-1990s, when the term "posttraumatic growth" was introduced by pioneering scholars Richard Tedeschi and Lawrence Calhoun. Posttraumatic growth occurs when a person utilizes hardships and life trauma to grow in their interpersonal relationships, spirituality, appreciation of life, personal strength, and, yes, creativity. This proved true for me on all fronts. I'm no longer the person I was before I lost my mother, my husband, and a grandson in the space of three years. In the seven years following my husband's death, I signed six book contracts, coordinated an annual grief retreat, became a public speaker and workshop presenter, established a large network of mentors and friends, and developed a personal relationship with God in the process. My husband foresaw the professional achievements, but no one who knew me just ten years ago could have predicted either the spiritual or the relationship changes—least of all me. Not when I'd been painfully shy for so many years, cultivating so few friendships.

"Creativity has the power to alter the darkness in our lives, whether we paint with it, draw with it, write with it, sing with it, work or play with it, or even just think with it," Gene Cohen says in *The Creative Age*.

I was driven to create in honor of those I grieved, not just in writing about them but in reaching out and encouraging others through workshops, classes, and public speaking. It seemed my heart had not just been broken—it had been broken wide open. When I spoke before a church congregation a year after my husband died, I discovered the authenticity that comes from personal experience. I began speaking on finding hope and faith in grief the following year. By 2017, I'd obtained certification for grief counseling. To this day, the comment I cherish most regarding my books and speeches is that people relate to me because I am "so real." I became a grief counselor because of my own pain, not in spite of it, aware that my own grief experience adds to my credibility.

While I'd discovered a way to utilize the emotional pain in my writing and speaking, grief did take its toll on me, and not just emotionally. I initially lost weight after my husband's death, but I soon gained it back, and then some. By early 2017, I weighed twenty pounds more than I had the day David died, five years before. My blood sugar soared, and I was plagued with anxiety. At my regular checkup, I told my doctor I feared I was so close to having a nervous breakdown that just one more thing might push me "over the edge."

"You're not going to crack," he replied, but a week later, I ended up in the emergency room with symptoms of a heart attack.

"Something has to change," he said, shaking his head.

Something did: I left the newspaper for the library position. Minus the anxiety that had become my constant companion, and with increased opportunities to practice creative endeavors, my load was lightened, figuratively and literally. I lost thirty pounds in five months, my blood sugar stabilized, and the anxiety receded. Not only was I feeling better, physically and emotionally, I'd discovered a sense of purpose in planning programs, writing, and speaking.

In her book *Finding Your Way in a Wild New World*, life coach Martha Beck describes awakening to her life purpose in adulthood as discovering her "rhinoceros." It's all about discovering whatever you should be doing with your life, what Beck calls your "true nature."

Beck believes her true nature was revealed by the age of four, when she spent her every waking moment immersed in the outdoors, watching birds and studying plants. "No one ever told me to think that way, to learn the names of several hundred mammalian species or to spend hours outside watching birds and munching random plants to see what happened. No one even urged me to read, but I did, obsessively, because how else could I travel to distant wildernesses, have great adventures, learn about animals I could never hope to see in real life? The great gift I got from my family, as the seventh of eight children, was the absolute freedom to read what I wanted, dive into any patch of wilderness I could find, and assume that I'd keep doing it my whole life," Beck wrote. "Unlike thousands of clients I've counseled in adult life, no one ever tried to stop me from following my true nature. Until I was five, anyway."

Beck was perplexed when she began attending school and discovered her teachers were not the least bit supportive of her dream to learn animal languages and live in the woods. It didn't take her long to realize that she needed to focus on her education if she wanted to succeed in today's world, and she did that quite well, attaining three Harvard degrees. Decades later, when she found herself face to face with a rhinoceros in the African wilderness, instead of fearing for her life, she was inexplicably happy.

"My life will have been worth living for this one moment, with these friends, this place, those primordial animals, this joyful pounding heart. I'm finding out what it feels like to reclaim my true nature."

Beck goes on to say that our "rhinoceros" can be anything that fulfills our life's real purpose. We'll repeatedly want to return to whatever it is that awakens such happiness in us. Maybe you already know what your rhinoceros is, or perhaps you have yet to discover your true nature, which is why our initial Ignite exercise was to look back to childhood. Your rhinoceros may be hiding there. Mine was. It doesn't take a stretch of the imagination to predict that the little girl who spent hours reading and scribbling out stories might someday become a writer herself. Nor is it difficult to imagine the high schooler who won awards at speech contests someday becoming a public speaker. Yet I didn't return to those roots of elocution for nearly forty years.

Whether it was cooking, gardening, spending time with animals, sketching, writing, empathetic listening, or music, there was something you were drawn to as a child, an activity that brought you joy, that you can reignite now, as an adult. Maybe your rhinoceros moment will come as you decorate a room, bake cupcakes, spend time with grandchildren, or work in the garden. Whatever way you add creativity into your life, you can be sure that living a more creative life is good for you. Research proves that.

In 2010, the *American Journal of Public Health* published "The Connection Between Art, Healing, and Public Health," a review analyzing more than a hundred studies regarding the impact of art on health. The studies included everything from music, writing, and dance to visual arts such as painting, drawing, pottery, and photography. They discovered that the practice of these various forms of art improved medical outcomes; reduced depression, stress, and anxiety; and increased social networks and positive identity.

So what are you waiting for? Maybe a little help finding that rhinoceros or picturing what your new creative life will look like?

A mind map serves as a visual thinking tool connecting information around a central subject. Mind mapping is a way to capture your thoughts and brainstorm ideas, utilizing both sides of your brain. The term "mind map" was first popularized by British psychologist and television personality Tony Buzan in the 1970s.

There are mind mapping apps and online tools, but for our purpose, you'll use the template included here. You can make other mind maps using a blank sheet of paper and pencils, pens, markers, or colored pencils. Adding color (or, if you are a very visual thinker, adding pictures) as part of your mind map helps free your creativity. But for this kind of brainstorming, you don't want to take a lot of time, or it slows down your thoughts and you start to censor yourself. Even if your initial thoughts don't make sense to you, include them—there's a reason those thoughts came to you. For this exercise, you'll design a mind map around the central idea of your more creative life. Begin in the center with "My Creative Life"; from that central idea, branch lines out to the areas of your life you want to concentrate on.

When I did one in early 2018, I decided I wanted to work on writing, public speaking, workshops, and personal goals. You may have more. From that central goal, branch out further, brainstorming ways to meet them. The farther out you go, the more creative your ideas will be. I noticed my ideas became more specific, as well. Not only did I want to increase my income and add more programs, mind mapping gave me the idea to add vision boards to my workshop offerings.

I've since made mind maps when I'm brainstorming ideas for a book, speech, or workshop. I drew a mind map while planning a workshop to teach authors how to create a program around their book's topic. I'm not sure I would have come up with the "3 E" idea of Educate, Engage, and Entertain without the mind map.

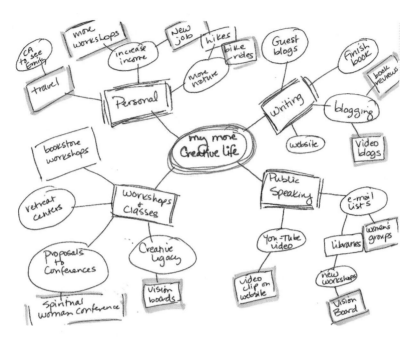

Mary's mind mapping exercise from February 2018.

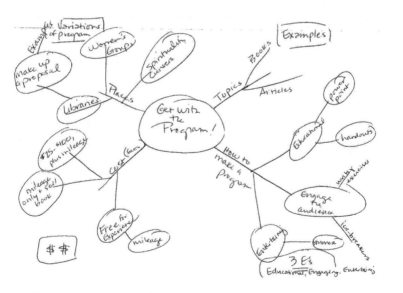

Mary's mind map when planning a "Get with the Program"
presentation for writers.

My Creative Life

Creative Spark:
STEVE POTTER

I moved into my brother Lyle's Cedar Falls home for three months during the summer of 1978, working at a local restaurant to earn money for college that fall. In between work hours and dates with the man who would become my husband, I often cared for my nephew Steve, a blonde-haired inquisitive toddler whose bright smile and gentle disposition won over my heart. Sometimes, as I pushed him downtown in his stroller to the nearby library, I pretended he was mine. We've shared a special bond ever since. Two years after that summer, I gave birth to my own towheaded son, Dan, who became good friends with his older cousin. We still lived in Cedar Falls when my second son, Michael, was born. By the time we moved away in 1992, Michael had his adored older cousin wrapped around his little finger.

"I do wish I could have that," little Michael would lament wistfully about whatever toy Steve had entertained him with during our visit, and kindhearted Steve would promptly give it to him.

There seemed to be one constant in my nephew's life outside of his generous nature: an interest in art. The toddler who loved to get ahold of crayons and paper was rarely seen without a pencil or other drawing utensil in hand. Steve is a perfect example of someone who has known what they want to be since early childhood, and his success is a tribute to his tenacity and drive.

"I have always felt the urge to draw and be creative. I never understood why more people didn't draw, because it came so easily to me," Steve says. "I was lucky to grow up in the 1980s with all that great nostalgia to feed off. When I was young, everyone said I was destined to grow up and work for Disney, but all I wanted was to draw demented art for *MAD Magazine* and Garbage Pail Kids."

In an article from his high school newspaper, Steve's art teacher was quoted as saying Steve was his own best teacher.

"I was always driven to do better and learn techniques to improve," Steve says. "My parents supported me with art supplies, and my mom even sent me to Des Moines a couple summers to stay with my Aunt Sara and take art classes at the Des Moines Center for the Arts."

Steve didn't have the heart to tell her that he hadn't really learned anything from the classes and was bewildered by the tours of the fine art galleries.

"I remember staring at a big white canvas with a thin red line drawn across it, with a price tag of $400," he says. "The class had continued on through the gallery, but I couldn't move from that spot. I just stood there staring at that piece of 'artwork,' trying to figure out the value in it."

In August 1999, 21-year-old Steve was diagnosed with a brain tumor and given a grim prognosis. Four rounds of chemotherapy and forty-four cranial and spinal radiation sessions later, he was left with peripheral double vision and nerve damage in his hands and feet. Though gripping a pencil hurt his fingers, he continued practicing the art that became a healing experience for him. His survival was the catalyst to begin attending art classes at a community college.

"I took every art class that was available, intermixed with my general studies: drawing, painting, 3D design, photography, film, and art history. They were so much fun," Steve says. "I was super excited to move on to a four-year university for what I considered the 'real' art classes."

Like so many creatives, he soon became disillusioned with the educational system. Eventually he came to the realization that it wasn't a degree he needed but a portfolio of artwork.

"I didn't fit in well with any of the teachers or students. I was instructed to 'stop working' right in the middle of paintings with large unfinished sections. I was told what to put together for art competitions." Steve shakes his head ruefully. "I was laughed at for getting too close to other people's artwork during critique time and instructed to totally change my style or I'd get a bad grade. I trudged through until the waste of time and money led me to drop out one credit shy of my fine arts degree."

He left school, but he didn't stop learning or creating. The nerve damage he'd experienced during cancer treatment eventually repaired itself, and he soon became known for his smooth linework. Steve continued aiming for the goal he'd had since the 1980s: to work on the popular trading cards from his childhood that had made a resurgence. His artwork appeared in many places: his beloved *MAD Magazine*, comics, custom tattoos, music CDs, books, clothing, and local businesses.

"I'm always doing random art. If someone needs artwork, I'll do it," Steve says. "Just the other day I was driving in the Industrial Park section of Cedar Falls where I live. I drove by three businesses I'd drawn the logos for."

Because of his love for 1980s trading cards and Garbage Pail Kids, Steve drew a lot of fan art, posting regularly on social media, eventually drawing the attention of the art director for the Topps Company.

"Their art director emailed me and asked if I would like to work on the actual cards," Steve marvels. "Of course, I said yes. I was so excited! It felt like a dream come true to work alongside the artists I'd admired as a kid. I became a fan favorite right out of the gate, and because of my high-quality work, Topps hired me on for additional brands, including Wacky Packages, *The Walking Dead*, and *Star Wars*. When Disney bought Lucasfilm in 2012, I could finally call my mom and tell her I worked for Disney! I've worked on around twenty trading card sets for Topps in the last six years."

In August 2012, Steve was diagnosed with a second, unrelated cancer in his salivary gland. Treated successfully by surgical removal, his health-related challenges didn't stop there. In April 2017, just a few months shy of forty, Steve had a heart attack.

"It threw me for a total loop," Steve says. "I got about six months behind on everything. I had to skip out on multiple trading card sets including *Mars Attacks*. It hurt."

The artist who'd finally managed to make a living off his art was forced to move to a smaller house and return to office work to supplement his income from the limited work he continues to do for the Topps Company.

"I'm just getting to a comeback stage where I'm drawing like crazy and having a lot of fun," Steve says. "My plan is to get back to drawing more art for myself. Just things I create for no other purpose than to spread my wings."

With that, all I can see is that bright-eyed little toddler I'd once yearned to claim as my own. And for a moment in time, he is.

Chapter 4:
BEYOND THE BOX

◆

make another trip to see her soon. First Mary will be having her 4th child and I will stay with the other 3 children. (Good way to get to know eachother!) Now, I've enjoyed being a daughter, tried to do my best as wife and Mother and like being a Grandmother. Think I'm an eccentric but like whatever I am.

◆

In the book *Breakpoint and Beyond: Mastering the Future Today*, George Land discusses his 1968 research study of 1,600 children who were enrolled in Head Start, the government-funded preschool program for children living in poverty that I attended in 1965. In that study, the children were given the test Land had devised for NASA to help select innovative engineers and scientists, measuring their ability to look at a problem and come up with new and different innovations. The same children were retested at ten years of age and again when they were fifteen. The results were astounding: 98 percent of the youngest children fell into the "genius category of imagination," but by the age of ten, that number was down to 30 percent; by age fifteen, 12 percent. Adults fared the worst. In 280,000 adults given the same test, a dismal 2 percent fell into the genius category. Land's conclusion was that we are born creative and that non-creative behavior is learned. What happens to children between the ages of five and ten? Despite the inherent value of an education, some might argue it is the school system itself that inhibits creativity.

Martha Beck, the author who wanted to learn animal languages and live in the woods, was not alone in discovering school had stifled some of her creativity. My nephew Steve found that university art classes did little for his imagination, and I remember the first time my natural creativity was squelched as a child—and it wasn't at home, where my mother snuck a Big Chief tablet into my underwear drawer to encourage my writing.

At five years of age, desperate to become a reader like my older siblings, I'd begged my sister Sharon to teach me. Instead, she read the same Dick and Jane reader aloud to me so many times I memorized it, learning to read the words by sight. To obtain the library card that was required to feed my new interest, I needed to be able to write both my first and last names. I practiced for hours until my handwriting was legible.

I skipped kindergarten altogether, beginning first grade already ahead of my peers. As a result, I was so bored, I'd pull books from the shelves near my desk and read them from my lap. When she caught me at it, the nun who was my teacher was furious I hadn't been paying attention to her phonics lessons, accusing me of "pretending" to read the book I'd hidden. I read a few sentences aloud to demonstrate my prowess, before she snatched it from my hands in exasperation, declaring I'd learned to read "wrong." I was confused. I'd sailed through the entire set of Dick and Jane readers and moved onto chapter books while my classmates struggled with the primer, yet I'd learned to read incorrectly?

Another milestone memory was in third grade, when I missed thirty-six consecutive school days due to illness and the teacher informed my parents I'd likely have to repeat the grade. I returned to school not only caught up with the work but once again ahead of the class. My dad had helped with the math, but I'd learned everything else from reading the textbooks that were sent home with my sister. I'm convinced those two formative experiences contributed to a disillusionment with the educational system and the foundation for a future homeschooling lifestyle.

After studying some of today's most creative minds, neuroscientist Nancy Andreasen, one of the world's leading experts on creativity, has pointed out that many of the people we consider to be creative geniuses dropped out of school. People such as Bill Gates, Steve Jobs, and Mark Zuckerberg were all self-learners, or autodidacts.

"Because their thinking is different, my subjects often express the idea that standard ways of learning and teaching are not always helpful and may even be distracting, and that they prefer to learn on their own," Andreasen wrote. They preferred figuring things out independently, "rather than being spoon-fed information."

Learning in school has typically depended on convergent thinking patterns, where students are instructed to follow a particular set of logical steps to arrive at the correct solution—which, as we've seen, is not particularly conducive to creativity.

"Our entire educational system is built on convergent thinking," Erwin McManus writes in *The Artisan Soul*. "Education has been reduced to the organization and dispensing of data. We teach our children that to excel in this world you have to be able to fill in the blanks. The worldview we transfer to our children is that there is always only one right answer to every problem, and that answer has already been discovered by your teachers."

Divergent thinking, on the other hand, focuses on spontaneous, free-flowing release of creativity and imagination to explore unknown paths and discover unexpected solutions.

Because I've covered school board meetings as a newspaper reporter, I've seen how school systems today struggle to address this dichotomy, offering STEM (science, technology, engineering, and mathematics) classes and opportunities for creative growth. I've also seen excellent and inspiring teachers fight the system to build innovative classrooms. But in 1991, when I observed my sensitive third child's personality change dramatically after he began junior kindergarten, I couldn't see many options. It was my mother who initially suggested homeschooling, but I resisted. At least until the parent–teacher conference when his teacher reassured me he was adjusting and had begun "kicking and screaming like the other little boys on the playground." That explained why gentle Michael had begun hitting his little sister at home. I promptly removed him from pre-kindergarten and his sunny disposition returned within days. That doesn't mean it was an easy decision. At best, I began as a reluctant homeschooler.

I made the radical move with a great deal of trepidation, worrying I might be performing some sort of grand social experiment with my family by pulling away from the formal educational system that had netted me a high school diploma and college degree. The negative peer group interaction that was breaking the spirit of my third child may have prompted the choice, but, truthfully, something about the practice had always intrigued me. I'd written a research paper on home education in college. The year before I joined their ranks, I'd interviewed several homeschooling parents for the local newspaper. Certain then that I could never do the same, I was still fascinated by the difference I saw in their teenagers, who hung out with their families, played with younger siblings, and seemed relatively unaffected by the peer pressure that had plagued me as a teen.

When I made the decision to remove my children from school, I read everything I could get my hands on regarding the various techniques of homeschooling, becoming increasingly enamored with the more "relaxed" methods. I worked with our certified teacher to combine real-life experiences, copious amounts of free time, and interesting books into a relaxed curriculum that included very few textbooks. By the time we had seven children, we'd moved to a house in the country, where my children spent hours in imaginative play.

In his teens, our homeschooled Michael would roam the woods with his dog for an afternoon, a can of beans and can opener in his backpack. He read every homesteading book he could get his hands on and completed two years of math workbooks in one summer. Rachel read voraciously, devouring books like they were chips from a Pringles can. She built a complex horse ranch on the online Ponybox game, getting so skilled with her herd she had members offering her actual cash to sell some of the imaginary horses to them.

Though our isolated lifestyle wasn't ideal for social skills, it had its merits. My rurally raised children became creative, responsible adults. In his early twenties, Michael purchased my mother's house, converting her workroom into his own. He now makes a living with the art he creates using the self-taught skill of glassblowing. Rachel has worked her way up in a job she's held since shortly after graduation, purchasing her own house before the age of twenty. The younger four, raised in town with more socialization opportunities, still carry fond memories of the days their older siblings entertained them for entire afternoons with elaborate puppet shows.

This is not to suggest every child should drop out of school or be homeschooled, but rather to demonstrate concrete examples of what it is to learn outside of a formal school setting, suggesting adults can do the same thing. Immersing oneself in a topic and doing extensive research for a book, learning glassblowing from YouTube instructional videos, or reading hundreds of books for enjoyment are all avenues to an autodidactic lifestyle.

I formed the creativity group at my library so I could connect with others who were interested in lifelong learning, forming a support system of sorts for a more creative life. Still, despite my eagerness to explore creative endeavors with them, my initial foray into playing a musical instrument convinced me I probably wouldn't become a musician anytime soon. As my fingers clumsily moved from a C to a G formation on the fret of the ukulele, a familiar feeling of embarrassment crept over me, threatening to ruin the experience. Then I looked up and met the amused eyes of another woman who was struggling just as much, and we both laughed, shaking our heads. We might not be musically inclined, but we could still have fun.

Later, when our group discussed bringing in an art instructor to guide us in a painting activity, the woman sitting next to me practically jolted out of her chair.

"What? Painting? We're going to paint?" her voice rose in panic. "I can't paint!"

"I haven't touched a paintbrush for forty years," I attempted to reassure her. Several others chimed in.

"I've never painted either," one said. "But I want to try."

"If it doesn't look like you think it should, tell everyone it's supposed to look like that. It can be an abstract painting," another commented with a laugh.

Our fearful member visibly relaxed with the reassurance, and soon we were talking excitedly about what we'd paint. It wouldn't be the typical "cork and canvas" type activity, where everyone drinks wine and paints the same picture. Instead, after an initial explanation of simple painting techniques, our instructor turned us loose, encouraging our group to paint whatever we wanted. Some came prepared with a picture they'd printed out. Others searched for an image on their phone. I'd decided on a bright, bold sunflower. When I dropped my paintbrush on the canvas, the single sunflower became two, and when that made the whole thing look off balance, I added another. My brushstrokes were hesitant at first, until I remembered what I'd read in the book I'd recommended to the group before our painting session.

"The joy is in the process. The joy is in the messy, the gorgeous, the ugly, the mistakes, the success, and the feelings of how great it is to express yourself," Rebecca Schweiger says in *Release Your Creativity*. "If you make the creative choice to practice a less judgmental attitude, you immediately welcome more inner peace and joy into your painting as well as into your life canvas."

Recalling those words, I made the conscious decision to just have fun, emboldening my strokes. Unlike my clumsy efforts with the ukulele, my fingers seemed to recognize the feel of a paintbrush. I soon discovered I preferred the more expensive paints the instructor had brought, offering a texture I desired. I added subtle notes of orange and brown to the thick strokes of bright yellow.

The completed painting looked nothing like I'd imagined, but even my untrained eye could see the possibilities, and I was eager for our group to do it again, though I'm not sure all the members shared my enthusiasm. One multitalented and particularly perfectionistic member wanted to abandon her painting altogether midway through our gathering. Others found painting as frustrating as I'd found ukulele playing to be, fearful of looking foolish.

Why are so many of us afraid to try new things? One of the biggest reasons seems to be a fear of failure.

"By leaving the 'tried and true' pathway of action or thought, the individual exposes herself to possible failure and ridicule. That exposure is very anxiety-provoking for many people," Harvard psychologist Shelley Carson writes in her book *Your Creative Brain*. "People say 'I'm not creative,' but that's just not true. Every one of us is creative. The brain is a creativity machine."

"How will I know if writing is my talent?" my daughter Katie asked when she was seventeen.

My answer came not only from the heart of a homeschooling mother who has always taken pains to encourage her children in their natural gifts but from an experienced writer who has faced repeated rejection. Writing for publication is not for the fainthearted.

"You write, and you submit, if you think that's what you'd like to do. But you don't let one rejection, or even ten, stop you if you think writing might be your calling. If you're drawn to it, then write," I told her. "Take classes, take workshops. Try different things, and you'll discover where your passion lies."

When we're seventeen, the possibilities of career choice can feel overwhelming. At seventy, if we haven't yet accomplished whatever it is we are "called" to do, we might think it is too late. After all, any craft takes time and work to develop, perhaps as many as ten thousand hours to be perfected. In his book *Outliers*, Malcom Gladwell popularized the "magic number of greatness" to achieving expertise in any skill as a matter of practicing ten thousand hours. Those numbers can be just as daunting at age seventeen as they are at age seventy.

"I don't know if I have ten thousand hours left," a woman in her seventies lamented during one of my Beginning Writing classes. I reminded her that the hours she put into writing as a child, as a teen, and into adulthood counted. She's not starting from scratch, and even if she were, she shouldn't let that stop her.

We shouldn't expect our first attempts to look like our final successes. So many of us try something new only to abandon it because it doesn't "look right" (or, in the case of my ukulele playing, sound right). There is intrinsic value in the attempt to stretch our imagination. The pursuit of a creative endeavor has merit even if it never becomes a career. We should give ourselves permission to draw because we enjoy it, paint because we find it relaxing, or write when we feel led to, whether or not we are "good enough." Simply allowing time for it in our life can be transformative.

"Each of us possesses a creative self. Claiming that is a transformational act. When you begin to act on your creativity, what you find inside may be more valuable than what you produce for the external world. The ultimate creative act is to express what is most authentic and individual about you," Eileen M. Clegg writes in her book *Claiming Your Creative Self.*

The truth is, while I enjoyed my ukulele-playing session, I'm not that interested in playing a musical instrument. I don't want to learn to read music, and I don't have a deep-seated desire to be a musician. Failure is always an option when we try something new, but at least I tried. I don't need to wonder if there was some hidden musical talent within me. There isn't. But I've always wanted to be a writer, ever since childhood. From that Big Chief tablet left inside my underwear drawer to the hours I spent in the local library, I can't remember a time when I didn't want to be an author, so that's where I've concentrated my ten thousand hours.

This book began as a formal book proposal, a boxed-in version of what I thought my publisher might want based on my other books with the same company. It was a perfectly acceptable proposal, stemming from an idea I'd had months after my mother's death. The format of the chapters and manuscript would have resulted in a book that looked much like my previous five. Christopher Robbins, the publisher, held on to my proposal for several weeks in relative silence before emailing to set up a phone call.

"I think we need to be more creative about a creativity book," he began our phone conversation. Essentially, I'd put the creativity book inside a self-contained idea box, and Christopher had taken off the lid. Suddenly, with his permission and a shared vision for a creativity book, ideas flowed seamlessly. That's what can happen when we open up our minds.

Begin your own creativity journey by taking the lid off the box you've contained your ideas and dreams inside. Once you do, you might be surprised by the imaginative world you find yourself in.

IGNITE

"Tell me, what is it you plan to do / With your one wild and precious life?"
—*Mary Oliver*

My mother made scrapbooks from brown paper sacks, pasting magazine pictures of things she'd like to make someday onto the pages. She kept another notebook filled with ideas for home decorating. A collage of what I want in my life would inevitably include overflowing bookshelves and stacks of stationery—simple things that make me happy.

What do you envision for your life or future? What do you want to surround yourself with? What are your hopes and dreams? Look back at your mind map for ideas. Create a "vision board" alone or with a group. Tear or cut pictures and inspirational quotes and words out of magazines. You can use some of the inspirational sayings included in the back of this book. Arrange the words and pictures on poster board or pick up a bulletin board at a thrift store, like I did. The black frame looks nice on a wall where I can easily see it, and I like the idea of being able to add to or change the layout. On my first vision board, I used a Bible verse as my focal point, adding a blue butterfly that represented the husband who'd encouraged me to fly. I wanted more nature in my life and yearned to see a mountain, so those pictures were added too. A member of my lifelong learners group decided to put together a vision binder instead. Choose what works for you. What does your creative future look like?

Mary Potter Kenyon's vision board.

Creative Spark:
GARY AND DEANNE GUTE

While doing research for this book, I stumbled upon a quote about midlife creativity from a professor at the University of Northern Iowa, my alma mater. When I searched the university's website to see if Gary Gute was still there, a 2013 headline popped up. Apparently, Gute was director of a new center aiming to "engage and inspire" faculty and students in the study of creativity. The center has since transitioned into the Human Potential Project, with Gute and his team continuing to help students discover their creative potential and offering them the latest research tools, opportunities for interdisciplinary and faculty-student collaboration, and exposure to renowned scholars, educators, inventors, artists, and entrepreneurs via campus conferences.

What I discovered about Gary during an initial interview led to a second one that included his wife, Deanne. Together, they were a prime example of a "creative spark couple." Not only had they founded the original creativity center while maintaining other full-time campus jobs, they lived an extraordinarily creative life outside of the university.

The two met as undergrads at UNI, while working as writing tutors. They soon learned they shared other common interests: an inborn fascination with old stuff and a love of history and good stories, dating back to their respective childhoods. A young Gary had collected classic records and books, while Deanne had nagged her parents to purchase old two-story houses, yearning for the creaky wood floors, attics with hidden treasures, and upper-story casement windows she'd read about in books.

After obtaining their master's degrees from UNI, the two attended Iowa State University to pursue their doctorates. It was no coincidence that both their dissertations were related in some way to creativity, as they each had studied Mihaly Csikszentmihalyi's concept of flow, experiencing that sense of losing themselves in their varied interests. Deanne's dissertation looked at bridging educational philosophies through informal learning, everyday aesthetics, and flow. Gary fortuitously ended up working with Csikszentmihalyi on his dissertation, and the two began actively collaborating on several projects on creativity, complexity, and flow.

"I doubt we'll ever solve the mystery of creativity," Gary says of the partnership with his mentor. "But I have some hope that we can contribute to a better understanding of it and help people cultivate it in their lives."

One area where Gary and Deanne discovered their mutual flow state is in house restoration, beginning with their Waterloo 1920s house with a huge park-like yard. They learned on the job with this first project, decorating and furnishing on a low budget, with limited skills and the guidance of *Old House Journal* and *Colonial Homes* magazines.

The next house, in Traer, came with the builder's Civil War diaries and an affordable price. Moving to the 1874 Italianate-style house was a no-brainer for the couple.

"We could step back in time over a hundred years and gain three times the space," Deanne says. "All we had to do was commute twenty-five miles to our jobs, leave the house we'd just finished, and take on all the new projects that dwarfed our first one in scale and complexity. It was worth it, because the house projects have also been all about revealing hidden potential."

They sought out mentors who would share their knowledge and inspire them with examples of house projects. They also helped plan and organize old house fairs in Traer and Waterloo.

"Through our old house work, we keep residence in two different worlds," Deanne muses. "There is the realm of books, students, theories, and research, and then the random—orbit sanders, scrapers, paintbrushes, solvents, and high-dust manual labor. For me, learning to strip and sand things and do physical labor gave me the one form of exercise I truly enjoy, along with a sense of strength and competence. It helps me carry on the DIY spirit my parents instilled in me growing up. And restoration also provides endless venues for thinking about color, design, and creative ways to bring ideas to life within a restricted budget. I believe a strictly digital, office-bound life is not a balanced one."

The home restoration does more than provide an exercise program. It feeds their creativity and passion for retaining beautiful and well-made craftsmanship. That means when Gary came across a homeowner who was burning parts of an 1860s house similar to their Traer home, he asked if he could salvage the parts instead. The portico slated for destruction was repurposed and attached to their house as a new "original" front porch.

"Creativity often means going against the cultural grain," Deanne says. "In our small way, we're trying to stem the tide of ugly, sloppy, contemporary building trends, our culture's taste for ease and comfort, and pressure from contractors who would rather trash old structures than invest the effort to renew them."

Besides their current Traer house, as time and money allow, the couple also works on an 1893 house that they eventually plan to move into. Originally built by a Waterloo doctor as a three-story brick home with a tower, they couldn't resist the rich history behind a house that used to occupy an entire city block, had once been relocated by horse power, and lost its tower and third floor in a fire caused by dried hydrangeas thrown into a first-floor fireplace.

"I think of the house and grounds as my sanitorium," Deanne says. "It only takes a few minutes on the property to feel stress levels abate and creativity surge."

"A musician must make music, an artist must paint, a poet must write, if he is to be ultimately at peace with himself. What a man can be, he must be."

—ABRAHAM MASLOW

Chapter 5:
HOME MATTERS

◆

Clothes were passed down in the family or to poorer relatives. When use of clothes was done, the best parts still made quilt pieces, doll clothes, sometimes even the doll, pot holders, strip rag rugs, handy rags and everyday hankies — there were no paper towels or Kleenex tissues.

◆

That first half-hour of every day is sacred to me. Perhaps it's a throwback from all those early morning hours of writing before children were up, but if I don't take time for a cup of coffee and reflection first thing, the day inevitably goes downhill from there. That time might include reading from a devotional, writing a letter, journaling, or—on really good days—working on an essay or book. It isn't just the solitude I cherish, but also my surroundings.

While I no longer have a separate office, I do have my own "space," a back room that spans the entire width of the house and serves as both bedroom and office. The bedroom portion is sparse; an end table and twin bed topped with a mockingbird quilt that matches the curtains. Outside of a washer and dryer in the opposite far corner, the rest of the large room is designed around the comfy brown recliner my children gave me for Christmas. When I sit in it to write or read, I'm surrounded by things that bring a smile to my face.

There is the Shaker-style cabinet I inherited from my mother, filled with things I treasure: my collection of autographed books, a hand-blown glass turtle my son Michael made, a toy sheep from my childhood, and bricks my daughter Rachel painted to look like the covers of my books. My grandmother's trunk is topped by one of Mom's quilts and her hand-carved Saint Michael statue, his sword upraised in regal glory.

Walls are adorned with paintings by my mother and daughter Emily, along with photographs taken by my son Dan, one framed and another on canvas. A rustic wooden rack is attached to one wall, the wire baskets holding stationery and greeting cards. Wooden letters with the cover designs of my six books on another wall spell the word WRITER, handmade by my daughter Elizabeth. Finally, there's a book-themed lamp atop an end table Katie painted to look like book spines. This is the environment that inspires me to write, a constant reminder of the creative people I love.

"We need to surround ourselves and our families with objects and ideas and activities that please and excite our senses, that make us smile, that provide a soothing balm of comfort for our days," artist Thomas Kinkade wrote in *Lightposts for Living: The Art of Choosing a Joyful Life.*

Evidently, from the notebooks and scrapbooks she left behind, my mother dreamed about doing just that. *Dream on*, she'd written on the front cover of a steno book where she'd glued pictures cut from magazines and jotted down notes, envisioning color schemes, textures, and furniture she liked. Like a vintage form of Pinterest, she'd glued pictures of fabric and wood project design ideas onto the pages of crude scrapbooks made from cut-down brown paper bags sewn together with yarn. Was "dream on" also her way of acknowledging the unlikelihood of ever acquiring those things? The sad irony was that until the last year of her life, when my sisters and I painted her walls with the colors she'd long desired, she'd only dreamt of having the woodsy moss, brown, and other hues of nature in her surroundings. She couldn't afford a redecorating project otherwise. Still, she'd managed to incorporate many of the art and craft projects she'd envisioned into touches of beauty in our simple home.

Mom was the epitome of the word homemaker, literally "making a home" in the apartments and houses wherever we lived. She embraced the domestic skills of sewing, baking, quilting, soapmaking, and canning produce from the gardens my father tended. She seemed to have a natural flair for color and design that she later applied to her painting and wood carving.

While much of the craft work my mother accomplished early on in marriage was utilitarian—rag rugs that covered areas of old linoleum, patchwork quilts that kept her family warm at night, toddler denim jumpers designed from a worn-out skirt—other crafts were strictly beautifying, like the bright scraps of extra material, buttons, and burlap bags she transformed into colorful wall hangings. Mom wouldn't waste even the smallest piece of fabric, using worn material or pantyhose to stuff a rag doll, cast-off woolen coats for teddy bear bodies, and extra quilted material for Christmas stockings with our names embroidered on the front.

Apparently, I hadn't inherited my mother's flair for color and design. The girl who'd skipped home economics classes for art and drama did not take up knitting or sewing when she got married. As two college students struggling to make ends meet, a serious lack of funds meant our home décor was more of an "early morning garage sale" theme.

That didn't change much after I abandoned the pursuit of a master's degree in family services to care for my own growing family. By 1988, as the mother of four children, my creative bent was aimed at writing, not homemaking, though I certainly became adept at combining sale prices with coupons, holding reign as the local coupon queen for many years. Less than ten years later, in 1996, we had six children and I'd added homeschooling and a home business to an already full life. An article I had published that year in the now-defunct *Home Education* magazine was aptly titled "The Messy Homeschooler."

I rarely invited anyone over; my home was always in disarray. A photograph from that year reveals that a visitor stepping into my house would have been greeted by the sight of a large wooden desk overflowing with the detritus of my lifestyle. Every inch of the desktop was filled: small bins held carefully organized refund forms and premium offers with corresponding proofs of purchase clipped to them, stacks of coupon inserts lay waiting to be clipped, carefully compiled lists of books I sold as a home business were ready to be folded and stuffed into envelopes. Boxes of books to be priced surrounded the desk, with piles sorted for mailing on top of those. In one picture, a canister of baby powder is perched on a pile of books, a baby carrier visible in the corner of the photo. This was my reality: the house where I juggled babies, bills, and business.

I'd consult my dog-eared copy of Peg Bracken's *The I Hate to Housekeep Book* or the self-proclaimed Slob Sister team in *Sidetracked Home Executives* for housekeeping hints. I desperately craved a well-organized space, a semblance of control over my house. I'd read every home organization article and book I could get my hands on, intent on getting my house in order. But for all the books I read back then, all the bins and baskets I'd purchased, I resembled the before version of the Slob Sisters more than I cared to admit.

At the same time, I was drawn to books like Alexandra Stoddard's *Living a Beautiful Life*, enamored with her descriptions of what a home should look like, how it should reflect its inhabitants. Ours did; it was a magnificently messy house full of imaginative children. While my heart desired control, our lifestyle invited chaos.

Like my mother before me, I still managed to find small, inexpensive ways to incorporate color into our home: a coat of fresh paint would do wonders for a boring white wall, a garage sale scenic picture brought the beauty of nature inside. Moving my work desk to a corner of the dining room meant visitors wouldn't immediately be greeted by the sight. Decorative baskets filled every corner, a valiant attempt to contain the overflow of toys and books. That was the extent of what we could afford in the way of redecorating. Photos taken in my parents' home in 1967 revealed much the same, with holes in the linoleum and torn fabric on the arms of chairs. Though they did little to disguise the obvious poverty, the braided rugs and colorful wall hangings went a long way in making the house feel like a home. The biggest difference was that my mother had handcrafted the bright spots in the dinginess of her poverty while I acquired mine at garage sales and thrift stores.

"The home we have right now can be perfect for us in this season. It's where we can find joy growing in our ability to manage and beautify what we have in a way that reflects who we are today," Melissa Michaels says in *Love the Home You Have*. "Art is a process. And like anything beautiful and worthwhile in this world, it takes time."

Simple functionality fit our needs during that season of life. We had food on the table, comfortable furniture, end tables that were happily and haphazardly strewn with books—along with half a dozen bookshelves filled with more—and plentiful paper and craft materials. My children were well-clothed, thanks to the bartering I did with the books I sold as a home business. They were fed, warm, and relatively happy. In the end, that's what really mattered.

By the year 2000, when our seventh child, Katie, was born, we'd moved to a house in the country and our finances had improved slightly. I attempted some rudimentary redecorating then, cobbling together a rose-themed bathroom and a bright apple kitchen in our rental home. I discovered ways to make a room feel cozier: a pretty comforter on a bed or a pop of color from a pillow. A separate office where I could stash much of the home business and homeschooling paraphernalia meant more room for hosting family get-togethers, my larger house becoming a gathering place. My home was a work in progress as I raised young children.

When we purchased our first house in 2008, I began systematically acquiring pieces of furniture, pillows, wall hangings, and curtains that matched, in colors and designs that brought me pleasure. Yearly tax refunds funded home improvement projects like new countertops and floor tiles for the kitchen.

Either I was a late bloomer or I'd just been too busy raising a family and struggling to make ends meet to make home decorating a priority before that. Author Eileen M. Clegg would likely agree it was the latter.

"Each person has a unique creative sensibility, but that can so easily become buried beneath the stresses and responsibilities of adult life. Sometimes a reawakening slowly occurs by one taking hold of a thread of something that's linked to something that remains pure inside each of us, a longing for expression, safe from the judgements or order imposed by the external world," Clegg writes in *Claiming Your Creative Self.*

My "reawakening" seemed to begin with my mother's cancer diagnosis, when I purchased a large rustic "LIVE" sign. Yes, there was the underlying message that I desperately wanted my mother to live. Yet, watching her face death so bravely, I was struck with a renewed sense of just how precious life is. I'll never forget Mom's smile when she spotted the sign hanging in my entryway or her apparent approval of the decoration and the message.

That simple wooden plaque was just the beginning in a series of steps to surround myself with color and comfort during a bleak time. Of course, I needed to paint the wall before I hung it up, and the new color led to replacing other pictures, which then required new drapes to match. It helped that I was working part time at my sister's consignment store then, so I had the opportunity to experiment with my sense of style using the wide variety of household decorations consignors brought in.

Shortly after Mom died, I purchased a matching "DREAM" sign, daring to dream I could honor her life through utilizing my talents.

That's exactly what I did the following year, by deciding to take my writing seriously and, as my husband so aptly worded it, began "flying and soaring" in my creative endeavors. When David died in 2012, I entered a period I can only describe as a dark night of the soul. Having lost the person I loved most in the world, I clung to writing and journaling like a lifeline, instinctively nesting in a pile of papers and books on the couch where I spent most of those first few weeks, occasionally glancing up from my frenzied writing to reflect on the meaning behind those two words on my walls: *live* and *dream.*

"Our immediate environment is one large part of our lives we can control. How we nurture our lives through the choices we make about where we live; the mood, spirit, and energy of our house; the rooms we decorate and occupy; the food we eat; the rituals we perform; the clothes we wear; and the colors we select to uplift us, make up approximately half of our happiness," Alexandra Stoddard writes in *Choosing Happiness: Keys to a Joyful Life*. "If we can improve our well-being by 50 percent, we should concentrate at least that much of our efforts on our external world, the one world we occupy by ourselves, the place where we live."

Whatever the season of your life, the home is the perfect place to begin practicing creativity. When opening our minds to the possibilities of what we can accomplish with our creative sensibilities, we need to address the physical space we inhabit, to make it conducive to inspiration. Surrounding ourselves with things we love contributes to our happiness and creativity.

Too many "things," on the other hand, can do the opposite.

According to a March 2014 *Los Angeles Times* article, the average US household contains 300,000 objects, from paper clips to ironing boards. That's a lot of "stuff." And, while I somehow managed to create amid clutter during those early years of parenting, there's no doubt that messy desk area contributed to my stress level. I was a much more productive writer once my children were older (and less messy) and my office area didn't serve double duty as a playroom too.

A March 2012 article on PsychologyToday.com cites seven reasons why messy rooms contribute to higher levels of stress hormones in our bodies. Clutter bombards our minds with excessive stimuli, distracts us, makes it difficult to relax, causes anxiety and feelings of guilt and embarrassment, inhibits our creativity and productivity, frustrates us when we need to locate something, and, finally, something I always considered was the very definition of motherhood, constantly signals to our brains that our work is never done.

Marie Kondo, founder of the acclaimed KonMari Method and author of *The Life-Changing Magic of Tidying Up* and *Spark Joy*, suggests discarding everything in the house that doesn't bring joy.

"Hold each thing you own in your hands and ask yourself whether or not it sparks joy," Kondo advises. "Then cherish the ones that you decide to keep, just as you cherish yourself, so that every day of your life will be filled with joy."

"When you wear and surround yourself with the things you love, your house becomes your own personal paradise," Kondo claims. In the thick of writing this book, I read both her books and a lively little tome called *The Gentle Art of Swedish Death Cleaning* by Margareta Magnusson. The author, self-described as somewhere between "eighty and one hundred," discusses death cleaning, or *döstädning* in Sweden. The term describes removing unnecessary things to make your home nice and orderly, saving heirs from a mess to deal with after you are gone.

"It is a word that is used when you or someone else does a good, thorough cleaning and gets rid of things to make life easier and less crowded. It does not necessarily have to do with your age or death, but often does," Magnusson writes. "Sometimes you just realize that you can hardly close your drawers or barely shut your closet door. When that happens, it is definitely time to do something, even if you are only in your thirties."

"Death cleaning is not about dusting or mopping up; it is about a permanent form of organization that makes your everyday life run more smoothly," she adds.

Facing an upcoming move in the spring of 2018 seemed an ideal time to streamline my own 300,000 possessions, putting into practice the advice I'd garnered from both decluttering gurus. It would be impossible to fit all the "stuff" from my four-bedroom, two-story home into a house with less than 760 square feet. I had to be brutal in the downsizing.

I started in my office, touching each item as I asked myself if it brought me joy or would fit in my smaller space. Did I really need two vintage blue Royal typewriters for display, or was one enough? What about wooden chess and checker sets that for the past ten years had hung on the wall gathering dust? My huge oak desk had to go and my desktop computer with it. I sold two solid oak bookshelves, weeding my book collection from over a thousand books to just those that would fit in the top two shelves of the vintage cabinet I was determined to take with me. Call it what you will, KonMari or death cleaning; in a purging frenzy inexplicably timed within thirty days of the deadline for this book, I got rid of half of my possessions, holding two garage sales and carting leftovers to the local thrift shop. In one final heartbreaking moment, I made the decision to give away my mother's table. There was no getting around it: my new kitchen barely had room for the small IKEA folding table the previous owner left for me.

My sister Angie lightened my load of sadness over the loss by joking it was now a "traveling table," going from one sister to the next as the need arose. Mom's table had come to me when this book idea was ignited. Angie picked up the table the same week I submitted the completed manuscript. It had served its purpose—it was time to let it go.

Though few readers will require getting rid of half their possessions in their quest for a more creative life, now might be the perfect time to address some clutter that may be inhibiting creativity and robbing you of joy.

"The ordinary arts we practice every day at home are of more importance to the soul than their simplicity might suggest."

—THOMAS MOORE

In the 1970s, my older sisters called them "Dust-Catcher Meetings," gathering at a friend or neighbor's home to trade things they no longer needed: magazines, paperback books, and decorative knick-knacks. Years later, my sisters and nieces occasionally met at my mother's house to do the same thing. My monthly lifelong learners group initially included a swap table, where craft materials, magazines, and household items could be traded with other members. Swapping items you no longer use is a "green thing," with community or private upcycling and recycling swap events taking off all over the county. Your challenge is to organize a swap party around something you find cluttering your home. Of course, this means your ultimate goal is to give more than you receive and donate anything left after the swap. You are defeating the purpose if you end up trading one material item for another. The idea is that by organizing this swap, you'll make a dent in your own clutter.

Use this handy checklist to organize your swap party:

- **Choose your swap theme:** What will you be trading? Do you have too many books taking up shelf space? Try a book swap. Want to purge your closet space? A clothing swap might be in order. Kitchen utensils, jewelry, purses; it's all fair game for swapping, and the swap can always be general household.

- **Send out invitations:** Who will you invite? Office mates? Friends? Church members? Your book club? You might want to try a smaller group your first time. Ten is manageable. For clothing swaps, you'll want similar sizes so everyone has something to choose from, but if you include purses and jewelry, then size isn't quite as important. Obviously, your book club would be interested in swapping books. It might be fun to send out paper invites, but you can always set up a private

Facebook event or group too. If you set up a Facebook group, entice invited guests with pictures of the loot you have to trade. What says "party" more than a great purse?

- **Set the ground rules:** Nothing bigger than a bread box is a good rule. No electronics or non-working items. No opened makeup. Clothing must be clean and free of stains or tears. Determine how many things each person can bring and how many they can take home. Since your purpose is to declutter, I wouldn't put a limit on how much leaves the house, but do take turns to make it fair, or one woman might grab all the purses and shoes and someone else be left with six pairs of sweatpants. Make it clear that unchosen items must be taken back home, but be prepared to take a load to your local thrift shop the next day regardless. If you were willing to swap it, you don't need it anymore. Get rid of it.

- **Arrange the swapping area:** Clear space, like your dining room table or the couch, for displaying the wares. Borrow some folding tables or a clothing rack if you need to. Serve refreshments. A tray of crackers, cheese, and fruit is always a big hit. Or make it a potluck, with everyone bringing a dish to share. They can even bring their contribution in a dish they're willing to swap!

- **Have fun!** You may find you want to do this on a regular basis. Someone's trash really is someone else's treasure.

Creative Spark:
SUE SCHUERMAN

Sue Schuerman is a talented writer, a leader of a monthly writer's group, a certified Legacy Letters instructor, and the co-coordinator of the Cedar Falls Christian Writers summer workshop, which is where I met this soft-spoken gentle spirit. I've never seen her frustrated or upset. She exudes calmness in every situation. After taking her "Dialoguing with Nature" workshop, I wondered if her relationship with the outdoors was the reason for her calm demeanor. It turned out that unique connection to nature stemmed from her childhood.

Born in Iowa, Sue's family moved to Florida, where her father and grandfather co-owned a gas station for several years. They returned to their home state in 1965, but not before those early years had a lasting effect on her.

"My happiest memories of those early years are at the beach and working in Grannie's garden. My grandparents' backyard was filled with ten orange trees, banana trees, a pecan tree, and lots of tropical flowers and a few veggies like tomatoes," Sue recalls. "My earliest memories of Florida are of tumbling in the salty waves of the Gulf of Mexico and emerging from the water to find seaweed tangled around my ankles, sand in my swimsuit, and salt in my eyes. I couldn't have been happier. The natural world has held a significant place in my heart and in my soul ever since."

Sue married Bill in 1971. The pair enjoyed camping and riding a tandem bicycle that accommodated their two children after they were born, with a backpack or children's seat. While her children were young, Sue did daycare in her home. Once they were in school, she took classes to become a medical secretary, working in that capacity for a few years before going back to college. She worked as Director of Volunteer Services and Community Relations for a care center for ten years before completing a human services degree at Upper Iowa University. She then served as Executive Director of the

Cedar Valley Arboretum and Botanic Gardens in Waterloo for five years. Even after she began work as Director of Communications for the UNI Foundation, she still found a way to incorporate a daily dose of nature by walking outside during her lunch hour no matter what the weather was like. She also walked three miles around Prairie Lakes in Cedar Falls three or four days a week.

Both avid photographers, Sue and Bill regularly visit lakes and forests around northeast Iowa. Sue has taken several nature retreats and classes on nature writing.

"Spending time in nature is a spiritual experience for me. As I tune into my surroundings, I often become aware of a wisdom that lifts my individual experiences into a greater experience of connection on the human level," Sue says.

Besides the health benefits inherent in walking and spending time outdoors, Sue believes her connection to the natural world is beneficial to her writing and photography. She is currently working on a memoir.

"I've been inspired to write a letter to a flower and an apology to a walnut tree. I like to think of my connection to nature as reciprocal and have created art projects from items found in nature. I then leave them in nature as a gift," she says.

Sue is intent on passing down that sense of awe to her grandchildren.

"It was after we had grandkids that we purposefully went on nature hikes and bird outings to teach them an appreciation of the natural world," Sue says. "We've done scavenger hunts, videos, night walks, and photo shoots with them. My youngest granddaughter and I always plant a fairy garden. I also did that with her older sister and brother. This is one of my favorite things to do because we're outdoors, using our imaginations."

Chapter 6:
AT THE SPEED OF TIME

around 1936

As soon as I could, I started climbing trees — my favorite place to read in Summer while enjoying the shade, any cooling breeze and a few curious birds. Sometimes I would just climb as high as I could to have a "bird's eye" view.

In hindsight, it was a bold move, writing a book on a topic I had so little personal experience with. I'd been teaching my own children for less than a year when I began writing *Home Schooling from Scratch*. Because I needed answers to homeschooling on a budget, I figured others would too. I went to the experts, collecting ideas and insight from parents who were already managing to save money in their choice of home education. The book was released in 1996, the same year I gave birth to my sixth child.

Up to that point, I'd managed to keep up with childcare, housework, homeschooling, and helping my husband operate our used bookstore. I was also bringing in a modest income with my extreme couponing and refunding, a home business, and freelance writing.

My first clue that my balancing act was off kilter was with my photo albums, or the lack thereof. This was before digital photos and discs took over, when our dating days, wedding, and family life were chronicled through plentiful pictures I'd carefully file in albums. Once Emily was born, all bets were off with photo archiving. I have yet to get a handle on what now amounts to more than twenty years of snapshots.

It was an era when "simplifying life" had become a national trend, with incredibly successful books like Sarah Ban Breathnach's *Simple Abundance* and Elaine St. James's *Simplify Your Life*. I read every book that celebrated slowing down to enjoy the simple things in life, along with dozens more on frugal living. I already lived the frugal lifestyle, raising a large family on a limited income. My mother and I were both charter subscribers to *The Tightwad Gazette* newsletter—and were even quoted in a couple of issues. It was the slowing down and finding abundant satisfaction in the process I found elusive.

The biggest problem was that much of the advice in the simplifying books didn't apply to me or my lifestyle. Reading them left me increasingly frustrated and, occasionally, furious. If I'd had the ability to spend even a fraction of the amount of time those authors seemed to spend on themselves, I wouldn't have felt overwhelmed in the first place. Who would be caring for my children, homeschooling, cleaning my house, and deal-shopping in the meantime if I was busy taking bubble baths, lighting candles, drinking copious amounts of tea, and experiencing that elusive solitude so conducive to creativity? How in the world did the authors have so much time to indulge on themselves? I was soon enlightened, discovering Ban Breathnach was the mother of one and St. James was childless. Where was the tome on simplifying life for women with large families? I decided I would write it and, in the process, help myself.

I turned to readers of two of my favorite magazines at the time, *Home Education* and *Big Happy Family*, running ads to request input from women who had four or more children. I planned the book's outline, devising a questionnaire that addressed all the big questions: how to organize a home filled with children, keep up with the laundry, live on a budget, handle sibling rivalry, and—the most crucial question of all—how to find time for the solitude and contemplation those other books recommended. I filled a file folder of information as letters from women all over the United States began to trickle in.

It was a novel idea: a guide to living the simple life for mothers of many. My tipping point came with the sixth baby, but surely there were mothers with slightly smaller or even larger families who also struggled to find time for themselves.

There were. I heard from dozens of them. The dilemma, outside of selling a book with such a limited audience to a publisher, was that while I garnered great ideas for sorting laundry and planning menus for larger families, I wasn't getting the answers I needed regarding time management or solitude. "Make sure to take time for yourself after you drop the kids off at school," was useless advice for a homeschooling mom. Even my own mother, with ten children, couldn't relate to the lack of solitude a homeschooling mother faced.

"Can't wait to read your book and get ideas," was the most common response to the question of how the respondents found time for themselves.

It wasn't long before I abandoned the book project altogether. It hadn't been a complete waste of time; I netted a wonderful pen pal relationship with a Minnesota mom who'd answered my call for advice. Pam was an aspiring writer and mother of ten. She was responsible for a piece of advice I would follow for the next sixteen years. Pam suggested I "take" (not make) the time I needed for creative endeavors, enlisting a friend, sibling, mother, or spouse to watch the children in my home while I left it to practice my craft of writing. I'd already been getting up an hour before anyone else every morning, but by following her advice and leaving the house once a week while my husband watched the children, I added two or three hours of uninterrupted writing time to my weekly schedule. That taken time didn't fill my photo albums, surely, but it definitely filled a well within my soul. Those stolen hours meant I was submitting at least one article or essay each week and getting published regularly in small magazines, couponing and refunding bulletins, and anthologies. For the next sixteen years, until my husband passed away, the only present I requested for Mother's Day was a gift certificate for a local restaurant so I could take myself out for breakfast and an extra-long writing session.

I never did discover the secret to solitude for mothers of young children, but apparently they aren't the only ones bemoaning a lack of free time for creative endeavors. According to the results of State of Create, a 2012 global benchmark study produced by the StrategyOne research firm, 52 percent of Americans report a lack of time as their biggest barrier to practicing creativity.

The single piece of advice on time management I garnered twenty years ago is the same I impart in my writing classes today:

If you are called to write, then write. Take the time. Don't wait for the perfect moment. If I'd waited to write until my children had grown up, I'd still be waiting. Time is not going to magically appear, and no one is going to give it to you as a gift (unless you ask for it for Mother's Day), so make the most of what little you have, even if it means writing by the glow of a nightlight or leaving the house for a morning. There will never be a perfect time to begin. All you have is now.

This advice could apply to any creative endeavor, not just writing. If you are called to something, find a way to fit it into your life.

"I am here to tell you with certainty: if you wait until you have a natural margin to create, you will go to the grave empty-handed. . . . If you are waiting for someone to beg you to do the work or promise to give you a huge paycheck or rearrange your schedule to clear the time or somehow make this whole part easier, you might as well take your little dream for a long drive into the country and say goodbye," Jen Hatmaker writes in *Of Mess and Moxie*.

My mother managed to produce a prolific amount of handiwork and art while she raised ten children. My binders filled with nearly thirty years of writing clips demonstrate that even without large blocks of time, I still accomplished a great deal of writing. In fact, I would argue that in practicing writing as a young mother, I acquired a skill set that has served me well: I can write anytime, anywhere, because I learned to tune out my surroundings. Just ask my children; each of them knows the blank look that indicates Mom is inside her head, not fully listening, whether I'm in the midst of a writing session or just thinking about a work in progress.

That's what author Manoush Zomorodi calls "spacing out" in her book *Bored and Brilliant: How Spacing Out Can Unlock Your Most Productive and Creative Self*. In 2015, Zomorodi, host of WNYC's popular podcast and radio show "Note to Self," led twenty thousand listeners to sign on to the Bored and Brilliant Project, an experiment to help them unplug from their devices, get bored, and jumpstart their creativity. "Mind-wandering" allows us to do some of our most original thinking and problem solving.

Dr. Jonathan Smallwood, professor of cognitive neuroscience and an expert in mind-wandering at the University of York, explains it like this: "In a very deep way, there's a close link between originality and creativity and the spontaneous thoughts we generate when our minds are idle."

I'd often let my mind wander in grade school, reading books from beneath my desk or staring out the window thinking about other things. "Mary has a problem paying attention," my fourth grade teacher had written on a report card that still reflected all As and Bs.

I continued my daydreaming through high school and into college, mostly about the man I was dating who would soon become my husband. David always seemed surprised when I'd hand him a letter or note I wrote during particularly boring lectures.

"Weren't you even listening?" he'd ask in wonder, knowing how well I did on the exams. He never understood how a girl who lived so much inside her head could function so well out of it. Years later, when I shared how I'd often silently narrate my own life (*Mary tentatively reached for the door handle, unsure what she would discover on the other side*), I was astonished to discover he'd never even heard of such a thing. I'd thought everyone did that to some degree. I remain a world-class daydreamer, some of my best ideas coming to me when I'm not trying too hard to bring them forth.

"Positive constructive daydreaming" was a revolutionary idea when Yale psychologist Jerome L. Singer began groundbreaking research on the topic in the 1950s. In a 2013 paper, "Ode to Positive Constructive Daydreaming," coauthors Scott Barry Kaufman and Rebecca L. McMillan review Singer's contributions to the research, looking at other supporting documents. They note that some people spend as much as 50 percent of their waking time daydreaming. Jonathan Schooler, another pioneer in the study of daydreaming, discovered that people who daydream score higher on creativity tests.

That's not to say that all daydreaming is created equal. The mind-wandering, daydreaming state that is most conducive to creativity is the kind that happens when you are mowing the lawn, in the shower, or taking a walk. It's the kind that author Brenda Ueland describes in her book *If You Want to Write: A Book about Art, Independence and Spirit*.

"It is the dreamy idleness that children have, an idleness when you walk alone for a long, long time, or take a long, dreamy time at dressing, or lie in bed at night and thoughts come and go, or dig in a garden, or drive a car for many hours alone, or play the piano, or sew, or paint ALONE. . . . With all my heart I tell you and reassure you: at such times you are being slowly filled and recharged with warm imagination, with wonderful, living thoughts."

For all the benefits of mind-wandering and daydreaming, there's no denying solitude enriches both. We need a semblance of quiet to hear all those thoughts banging around in our head.

"I learned . . . that inspiration does not come like a bolt, nor is it kinetic, energetic, striving, but it comes into us slowly and quietly and all the time, though we must regularly and every day give it a little chance to start flowing, prime it with a little solitude and idleness," Ueland continues.

Ah, solitude and idleness. I would have found this sort of writing advice maddening when I was the mother of young children. The words of acclaimed poet Mary Oliver convey the same need, in a more lyrical form:

"Creative work needs solitude. It needs concentration, without interruptions. It needs the whole sky to fly in, and no eye watching until it comes to that certainty which it aspires to. . . Privacy, then. A place apart—to pace, to chew pencils, to scribble and erase and scribble again."

I was pregnant with my fourth child when I submitted my first piece of writing. All it took was that $50 check and I was hooked, determined to beat the odds, to defy Virginia Woolf's famous quote, "A woman must have money and a room of her own if she is to write fiction." I had neither. How could I possibly write with three children underfoot?

Yet I did. I took the time. As did Harriet Beecher Stowe, who managed to write *Uncle Tom's Cabin* while raising seven children. Jodi Picoult began writing when she had three children under the age of four. J. K. Rowling was a struggling single mother when she penned *Harry Potter*. Madeleine L'Engle, author of the acclaimed *A Wrinkle in Time* and the delightful *Crosswicks Journals* series, learned to utilize snatched writing moments.

"To write consistently, I must seize opportunities. I write in airports. I write on planes. I find airports and planes and hotel rooms excellent places in which to write because while I am in them, I am not responsible for anything except my work . . . I am free to write," she shared in her book *Walking on Water*.

I wrote at five in the morning, before children were up. I wrote by the dim glow of a nightlight as my children fell asleep or on the lid of the toilet while toddlers splashed in the tub. I pulled over to the curb in an idling car while a baby slept in the backseat.

Now that I actually have a room of my own and periods of solitude, I see the value of it for another reason: it has been through solitude and silence that I've learned to listen to God. For me, art and faith are intrinsically linked, as they were for Madeleine L'Engle.

"And as I listen to the silence, I learn that my feelings about art and my feelings about the Creator of the Universe are inseparable," L'Engle wrote in *Walking on Water*. "To try and talk about art and about Christianity is for me one and the same thing, and it means attempting to share the meaning of my life, what gives it, for me, its tragedy and its glory. It is what makes me respond to the death of an apple tree, the birth of a puppy, northern lights shaking the sky, by writing stories."

The hours of solitude in my mother's empty house the winter after her death brought more than prolific writing. I also did a lot of praying in those quiet moments. My search for solitude seemed to overlap with my search for a relationship with God. Seventeen months later, during the early weeks after my husband's death, I was brutally thrust into a state of stillness, barely registering the passage of time in the fog of grief. I'd spend hours on the couch, surrounded by books and paper: writing, reading, praying, and wrestling with my thoughts. *What now? What do I do now, without David?* For the first time in my life, uttering those prayers of desperation, I learned what it was to listen for the answers.

"For I know the plans I have for you, plans to prosper you and not to harm you, plans to give you hope and a future." I read the Jeremiah 29:11 Bible verse repeatedly in devotionals.

Could it be true? Did God have plans for me? Had he gone before me, preparing me to be alone? Within that stillness, I felt the first stirrings of hope. I came to believe there was a divine plan in all of it, that I could build a new life from the ashes of what my life as David's wife had been. Following the promptings of the Holy

Spirit, one year after my husband's death I wrote a speech and designed a PowerPoint presentation to minister to the broken hearts of grievers, a ministry that would eventually propel me into organizing an annual grief retreat in my area and seeking certification in grief counseling. In quiet solitude, I discovered a calling in addition to writer: that of public speaker.

"When I am constantly running there is no time for being. When there is no time for being there is no time for listening," L'Engle said in *Walking on Water*.

From that place of grief-laden stillness, I had ample time for listening, planning, and creating. It seems a shocking thing to admit, but sometimes I miss the slowness of those early months of grieving, though certainly not the accompanying emotional pain. The challenge, then, is to incorporate some slowness into our everyday lives. One way to do that is by connecting with nature. Called the "tonic of wilderness" by acclaimed nature poet Thoreau, a natural setting is an ideal place for your mind to roam free.

According to an article in the December 2014 *Journal of Environmental Psychology*, research conducted by doctoral student Carmen Lai Yin Leong and her mentors at Victoria University of Wellington in New Zealand supports the theory that being connected with nature is associated with innovative and holistic cognitive styles.

Just taking a walk tends to improve creative thinking, whether the walk is indoors or outdoors. According to a study coauthored by Stanford doctoral graduate Marily Oppezzo and Stanford professor Daniel Schwartz, walking boosts creative inspiration.

"Many people anecdotally claim they do their best thinking when walking. We finally may be taking a step, or two, toward discovering why," Oppezzo and Schwartz wrote in the study that was published in the *Journal of Experimental Psychology: Learning, Memory, and Cognition*.

Consider making your walk an outdoor one. Research done by Marc G. Berman, John Jonides, and Stephen Kaplan of the University of Michigan demonstrated the restorative effects on cognitive functioning of interactions with natural versus urban environments. An interesting note: their research, reported in the 2008 journal *Psychological Science*, revealed that even viewing pictures of nature produced cognitive improvements.

Writing is very much an indoor activity, one that keeps me glued to the chair for more hours than I'd like to admit. When I took a "Dialoguing with Nature" workshop in the summer of 2017, it was an eye-opening experience for a woman who'd lost touch with the child who spent hours outside every day. As a youngster, before I was old enough to be assigned daily chores, I'd spend hours outside—poking sticks at anthills, creating mud pies with the dark, rich loam my father dug up in the garden, sitting in the hot sun wriggling my toes in the cool grass. The product of a Catholic elementary school and too many saint stories, I'd trek through the weeds in our small pasture to sit on a rock to wait for Jesus, Mary, or someone else holy to appear to me.

Through instructor Sue Schuerman's workshop, a part of myself that had been squelched by a sedentary writing lifestyle was awakened. It made me realize I didn't have enough nature in my life. I soon discovered a quick bike ride, or even something as simple as changing environments to sit on the back deck to write, could jump-start a stagnant mind. Spending time outdoors in the fresh air just makes good health sense, which is why our next Ignite activity takes place there.

"I lived in solitude in the
country and noticed how
the monotony of a quiet life
stimulates the creative mind."

—ALBERT EINSTEIN

IGNITE

This exercise is a modified version of Creative Spark Sue Schuerman's "Dialoguing with Nature" workshop.

Sue's directive:

Plan to do this exercise outside, with the natural world as your teacher. You will be utilizing meditation and contemplative writing in a nature setting. You can do this exercise alone or with a group. It is meant to quiet your mind, utilizing "contemplative writing to discover intimacy in your spirituality and soul."

Meditation:

Quiet your mind. As a child, we didn't have all the distractions we have as adults. I invite you to close your eyes. Breathe in the fragrances of the earth, letting it fill all the spaces of your being. As you exhale, feel the air cascading down through your heart and your lungs until it reaches your toes. Feel it ground you to the earth like the roots of a tree. Now let your mind return to a time in your childhood. A time when you felt connected to nature—through an animal, an insect, a lake, a garden. Stay in that moment. Drink in the joy. Feel the air moving around, breathe in the scents, see with childlike wonder the landscape before you. Now let yourself know that that child is still alive in you now. As we sit quietly, breathing in the common breath, feel the connection that comes from joining together. In this quiet place, you are that child once again. Now I invite you to slowly open your eyes and take that child with you as you go on a nature walkabout.

Writing Exercise:

What does this place awaken or stir in you?

_____

_____

_____

What do you notice about yourself or others in this place?

_____

_____

_____

_____

_____

_____

_____

What kind of awe or respect arises in you? How does it feel?

_____

_____

_____

_____

_____

_____

_____

_____

_____

_____

Creative Spark:
SUE ENGELBRECHT

In more than two hundred interviews I did for the newspaper, I'd never seen someone come prepared the way Sue Engelbrecht did. Pulling a piece of paper out of her pocket, she began reading off a list she'd taken the time to compile the night before. Her tally of life's most underrated pleasures included things like sun-dried sheets on the bed, the smell of freshly mown grass, the morning sun coming through the trees as she sat on the porch, a pair of comfy shoes, or that first cup of coffee of the day. Her eyes sparkled as she mentioned a restorative yoga class she attended and the gratitude journal she kept.

"When you have a grateful heart, it's hard to be negative," Sue said. "Surround yourself with positive people, with people who have the same passions. You can just feel the positive vibrations."

Then she turned the tables on the interview, handing me a piece of paper and instructing me to compile my own list.

"Life is a gift. No one is guaranteed tomorrow," Sue said when I reminded her of our first meeting. "We must always remind ourselves to live in the now."

After graduating from high school, Sue attended dental school to become a certified teaching dental assistant at the University of Iowa College of Dentistry in Pedodontics, which was where she met her husband, Daniel. She went on to become a nurse after he completed his dental degree. The couple had three children. Sue worked part time most of her nursing career after giving birth to the first of their three children, even though some years she put in a lot of hours in the OR and Recovery Room (now known as PACU, or post-anesthesia care unit). During the last ten years of her nursing career, she worked in outpatient cardiac rehab. When I interviewed her in 2015, she was nearing retirement.

At the time, I wondered how a woman with such a demanding career managed to be mindful with a busy schedule. Later, she shared how some pivotal moments in her past led to her life philosophy.

In November 1964, eleven-year-old Sue was in a car accident that took the life of her oldest sister, Joan. Her mother's example of faith in the face of grief helped Sue deal with the future losses of both her parents and two of her seven siblings.

"Saying goodbye to loved ones at an early age has shaped me and my spirit," she says. "God gives us one moment at a time."

Sue cherishes each and every one of those moments, appreciating the present.

"Every year on November 20th at 1:00 p.m., no matter what I'm doing, my world stops, and I feel my mom and Joan's love and presence," she says. "The tendency to live in the past can make one sad. Living in the future can cause anxiety."

Sue conditioned herself for joy by doing little things she loves on a regular basis, allowing for and appreciating the smallest pleasures in each day. Her enthusiasm is evident as she discusses her varied passions: playing guitar, singing, studying essential oil blends.

"Do things that inspire you. Know what you love, what brings you joy," Sue advises.

Two years after our initial interview, when I encountered Sue in the library where I worked, she mentioned her "Bucket List": the top fifty things she wanted to accomplish after her impending retirement. Her eyes lit up with excitement as she related some of them: learn to play the violin, become a Master Gardener, take a weaving class, attend a music camp in Tennessee, get a rock tumbler to polish rocks, and take a train trip to the Canadian Rockies. She added "join the library's lifelong learners group" when I told her about it.

Sue is one of the most vibrant of our group, exposing the rest of us to ukulele playing and hand-lettering. We have yet to introduce a topic that she hasn't at least dabbled in. She brings an enthusiasm that energizes the rest of us. Her joy and appreciation for life is contagious.

Two years after retirement, Sue has managed to check off the list many of her desired goals. Of course, ever the lifelong learner, she's also managed to add half a dozen new ones.

"The gift I treasure most is a good laugh. Laughter is the music of the soul," Sue says. "I keep a digital photo journal of all the 'wisdom gems' I've gathered over the years.

"When I get my new Apple desktop, I'm going to design photo family books to leave for my children," she muses, adding yet another goal to her growing list. "And a book filled with jokes and stories I've collected that have made me laugh out loud, for friends with terminal illness."

She chuckles good-naturedly. "I think my list needs to be renamed 'Sue's Perpetual Bucket List.'"

"Creativity can manifest itself anywhere, doing anything. Baking love into bread. Putting life's experiences into a novel. Singing in harmony. Going on stage. Growing a garden. Working with children. Painting dreams on canvas."

—EILEEN M. CLEGG

Chapter 7:

THE ART OF NOW

◆

How calm a walk through the woods can be. See the
beauty of snow as it falls or as it blankets the ugly.
Did the goodness of someone gladden your heart ?
Was there realized the miracle of a newborn baby?
a beautiful sunset ? a majestic storm or the roar
of the ocean and the smell of salt air ? the high of
music, the feel of the sun's warmth through a window
on a cold day ? a hint of the angels in the innocence
of little children (look at them as they're sleeping)?

◆

Having a very low-key morning so far. We never rush here. We do what the girls feel like doing. I felt a pang of envy as I read the letter my friend Mary had written during a visit with her daughter's family. When was the last time I hadn't felt rushed? The last time I'd spent an afternoon alone with my grandchildren? I continued reading: *We stay here to play if they want. Or take a walk downtown for hot chocolate and a muffin. Go swing on the porch or go to the playground or beach. There is so much to do . . . at a casual pace.*

A casual pace—sigh. It might come as no surprise that a woman who'd lost touch with nature and hadn't learned how to listen to God until after her husband's death might not have mastered the art of living in the moment either.

While an exact figure remains unknown, estimates as to how many thoughts we have each day range from 15,000 to as many as 70,000. Though faculty with the University of Southern California's Laboratory of Neuro Imaging have done some preliminary studies using undergraduate student volunteers, estimating 60,000 to 70,000 thoughts each day, or roughly 48.6 thoughts per minute, these results are not peer-reviewed or published. Accounting for the fact that most of these study results are rough estimates and there is no generally accepted definition of what a "thought" is, there's still no denying that we have a lot of stuff banging around in our head, scattered thoughts vying for our attention. Living in the moment isn't the easiest thing for the unpracticed among us. Easier perhaps for the meditative sort, like my letter-writing friend Mary, who seems to have perfected the art of relishing each precious moment spent with her grandchildren.

For a brief period after my husband's death, my default mode was living in the moment. A modest life insurance policy meant I could pay for the funeral, the burial, and a newer vehicle and still have enough left over to not have to work outside of the home for at least a year, maybe more. I recall the exact moment I made the decision to take advantage of that blessing.

It was only a week or two after David died. As I stood in front of the open kitchen window doing dishes (an activity particularly conducive to contemplation), I was startled out of my reverie by a group of birds congregating around the backyard feeder, chirping and squawking as if in accusation: *Where's our food?* The feeder was empty. It struck me then: David had been responsible for filling the bird feeder. Who would fill it now? I began crying, the wet and noisy sobs that erupt with fresh grief. *What will I do without David?* Not just regarding the bird feeder, but for the rest of my life? More importantly, what would David have wanted me to do?

The answer came easily. David had hated that I'd offer to cover stories for the local newspaper when I wasn't the least bit interested in them just because we needed the income. He'd lamented the writing time I lost when I pitched in to work at my sister's consignment store. I knew without a doubt that he wouldn't want me to be doing anything I didn't really want to do, just for money. That knowledge was strangely liberating. In an extremely uncharacteristic and somewhat selfish move, I made a life-altering decision. For at least one year, I would partake only in those activities I enjoyed that also allowed me to be with Abby, our youngest child. I informed the newspaper I wouldn't be doing any more freelance work and ceased working for my sister. Aware not every widow has that kind of option, I was grateful for it. I've never taken for granted or regretted that investment of the precious gift of time.

For nearly eighteen months, I spent most of every morning writing: journal entries, essays, articles, and a book that David had believed in. I traveled all over Iowa doing couponing workshops, once as many as fifteen in the month when my couponing book was released. Abby served as my travel companion, reading books in the children's area of the libraries we visited while waiting for me to finish presentations. I taught evening and Saturday writing classes and began public speaking.

I'd ride bikes with my girls and take leisurely walks to the library. Late in the day, I'd sit on my back deck and read or write. Yes, I was in mourning. Lone bike rides guaranteed a spate of tears (David and I had often ridden together), and I cried nearly every day before I settled in to write.

But losing the person I loved most in the world, a man who'd relished living after a bout with cancer in 2006, gave me a renewed appreciation for life. I'd lift my face to the sunshine, closing my eyes and soaking in the warmth. I'd savor the breeze in my hair when I biked to the cemetery and the smell of fresh-mown grass. Every scent seemed sharper, every color more vivid. I'd gasp at the beauty of a rainbow. Like the young bride who used to view her laundry drying on the clothesline, I'd watch the sun set on the horizon then get up early to see it rise. I'd found *hygge*.

Hygge, a Danish term pronounced "hoo-guh," has no direct English translation. Deriving from a sixteenth-century Norwegian term, *hugga*, which means "to comfort" or "to console," it perfectly describes the heightened senses and mindful moments that followed my husband's death, bringing consolation and healing.

The Danish define hygge as a quality of coziness that engenders a feeling of contentment or well-being, associated with relaxation, indulgence, and gratitude. Virtues of Scandinavian coziness have been extolled in many American books and articles in recent years. In *The Book of Hygge: The Danish Art of Contentment, Comfort, and Connection*, British–Danish author Louisa Thomsen Brits casts hygge as a state of mindfulness, demonstrating how to make mundane tasks more joyful.

Meik Wiking, CEO of the Happiness Research Institute and author of *The Little Book of Hygge*, discusses the link between hygge and happiness and outlines a hygge manifesto that includes good lighting and candles, comfortable and beautiful textiles, socializing, pastries, and hot drinks.

Much like the simple living books I'd once disdained, hygge as a life philosophy assumes a certain level of wealth and leisure time: hours spent with family or friends around a fireplace, icons of quality draftsmanship decorating one's surroundings, and copious mugs of hot tea and burning candles. As much as I needed the hygge lifestyle, it didn't pay the bills. A year and a half after David's death, I began searching for employment. I was lucky to land a library director's job that allowed for my daughter's presence and left mornings open for writing. With the newspaper reporter position some eighteen months later, I gained health insurance but lost both those perks.

When I returned to library work in early 2017, I spent the first week on the new job just decompressing, going through file cabinets and learning the ropes of a position that was as familiar to me as an old friend. Not only had I served as a library director; as a teen, I'd worked in my small hometown library, and I worked there again for a couple of years before Abby was born.

Observing my new coworkers, I noticed how hard they worked at their assigned duties—but at a pace that seemed almost leisurely compared to my newspaper colleagues who'd had breaking news to cover and pressing deadlines to meet. I could barely contain my excitement at the difference in my own duties of planning and implementing programs for senior citizens, visiting homebound patrons, and being surrounded by books and people who loved books. I felt my tight shoulder muscles relax, my jaw unclench. I could breathe again.

"Bringing our attention to the breath is a fast, simple way to ground ourselves in our direct experience of the present moment, to move into a more mindful state of being," Wendy Ann Greenhalgh writes in *Stop Look Breathe Create.*

That state of being, of living in the moment, is commonly referred to as mindfulness. On his website, Dr. Danny Penman describes it as "paying full conscious attention to whatever thoughts, feelings, and emotions are flowing through your mind, body, and breath without judging or criticizing them in any way. It is being fully aware of whatever is happening in the present moment without being trapped in the past or worrying about the future. It is living *in* the moment, not *for* the moment."

In his book *Mindfulness for Creativity*, Penman explains how mindful practices enhance three essential skills necessary for creative problem solving. Mindfulness switches on the divergent thinking that is so important to opening up the mind to new ideas. It improves attention, making it easier to register novelty and the usefulness of ideas. And finally, mindfulness nurtures courage and resilience in the face of skepticism and setbacks.

"Mindfulness" seems to be a catch-all term in the creativity discussion, often associated with the practice of meditation. Many artists, writers, and entrepreneurs have turned to meditation as a tool for enhancing brain function, improving the immune system, dissolving anxiety, stress, and depression, and tapping into their artistic mind to unleash creativity.

For all its perceived benefits, we can sit and meditate morning, noon, and night, extolling the benefits of daydreaming, mind-wandering, and solitude, but when it comes to creativity, at some point we need to focus on *doing*.

"The goal of a creativity mindfulness practice is not the non-judgmental observation of our thoughts but complete right thinking that leads to reams of writing and oodles of mental health. Our goal is not to be calm, centered, or even enlightened, but to be all of that and also to write like a wild person," Eric Maisel advises in *A Writer's Space*. "The central goal of traditional mindfulness is that when you eat a potato, you really eat that potato. The goal of creative mindfulness is that when you eat that potato, you really eat that potato and you also work on your novel."

In a nutshell, don't just rest and meditate; *do something*.

It could be argued that immersing oneself in writing or other creative endeavors and getting lost in the flow *is* the mindful practice. Drawing, painting, collage making, photography, journaling, and writing are all naturally meditative, calming the artist in creative mindfulness. Internationally renowned artist Rebecca Schweiger thinks so.

"Creativity is an active meditation where, through the act of self-expression, you learn to focus your mind, deepen your self-awareness, and let go of thoughts, feelings, and stresses while relaxing into a truer version of yourself," she writes in *Release Your Creativity*.

Wendy Ann Greenhalgh defines mindfulness in two ways in *Stop Look Breathe Create*: mindful *doing*—when we focus our breath, body, or sensory experience through a creative practice such as drawing, writing, or photography—and in simply *being*—being with each moment in our life without analyzing or thinking about it, open to the beauty of the world and our own creative nature.

I want it all. I want to write *and* to savor the beauty of each moment. I want the potato and the mindful eating of it—don't you? In order to have that, we need to slow down, learn to live in the now, and mindfully make cherished memories. In Barbara Bradley Hagerty's book *Life Reimagined*, she discusses scientist Carol Ryff's research behind frequently marking off mental milestones, suggesting that we should train ourselves to take mental snapshots of moments. By doing so, life feels as if it slows down, taking on more meaning. According to his published diaries, Charles Lutwidge Dodgson, better known as author Lewis Carroll, marked days he felt to be especially memorable as "white-stone days" in his journal, adopting the Roman symbol for a day of good fortune. Much like Sue Engelbrecht with her gratitude journal, I like to mark white-stone moments in mine.

"We rush around with our bodies tense and our minds whirring, ticking off things on our to-do list—picking up the kids, finishing that report for work, going to the gym or the mall or that long-distance meeting—winding ourselves up into such a maelstrom of busyness that we lose touch with the small and nourishing pleasures in life, the beauty and peace of the world around us, and the deep satisfaction of being playful and creative. All acts of mindfulness, creative or otherwise, start with pausing and reminding ourselves that there is another way: the simple act of being," Greenhalgh writes. After we pause, she suggests three additional steps to becoming more mindful: taking time to look around us, consciously connecting with our breathing, and beginning to create.

There are other ways to promote or enhance mindfulness. When the meditation comes in the *doing*, preparation could be quiet time reading a devotional or the Bible, a moment of prayer, a walk through the park, or a ritual of some sort that quiets the mind and soul.

I'd instinctively approached my winter writing sessions in my mother's empty house this way. Away from the cacophony of a house filled with children and the lure of the internet and housework, my internal clock quieted, slowing down. First, I'd clean the table, sometimes even taking the time to appreciate the play of dust particles in the rays of sunshine coming through the window. I'd set out a legal pad, pens, and my laptop on the newly shined surface.

I'd light a cinnamon candle and pop a Kenny G CD into the computer for easy listening. I was setting the scene for my writing session, the rituals calming my senses and relaxing my breathing. Only then would I begin to write.

I seem to have mastered the mindfulness I need to practice my craft. The challenge comes in applying the same principles to the rest of my life: learning to live in the moment or, as my friend Mary so aptly puts it, to "just be."

"Ordinary thoughts course through our mind like a deafening waterfall," biomedical scientist Jon Kabat-Zinn says, suggesting that, to find a sense of balance, we need to stop doing and focus on just being.

This is the sort of mindfulness we should strive for: awakening to fully experience life instead of letting it speed by. But how can we actively engage in moments of our life when there is so much clamoring for our attention or causing anxiety—jobs, or a lack thereof; bills; chronic illness in ourselves or someone we love; or caring for children, grandchildren, or even parents?

"I believe that our natural, mindful creativity should be the way we experience most, if not all, of our days. By engaging in some new activity—whether it is art, music, sports, gardening, or cooking—on an ongoing basis, we can begin to experience what it is like to be more mindful. Most of the time mindlessness comes by default, not by design, and when we are mindless we're oblivious to being so. We need to find a way to cue us into our mindlessness. We need a bell that will sound for us, signaling that we are acting mindlessly," Ellen Langer says in *On Becoming an Artist*.

What if that cue, the key to becoming grounded in the present moment, the *now*, is as simple as breathing?

"You breathe 22,000 times every day. How many are you aware of?" Danny Penman asks in his book *The Art of Breathing*. He argues that the answer to letting go and finding peace in a messy world is to take time to breathe.

The first time I heard the song "Breathe," by Jonny Diaz, I was in the car on the way to a newspaper staff meeting. My hands were clenched on the steering wheel, my monkey mind jumping all over the place, when the melody implored me to rest, and just breathe.

For the duration of the song, that's just what I did, arriving at the office a little less stressed, convinced there might be something to this breathing thing. From that point on, I treated the twenty-minute trip as an exercise in breathing, consciously taking in deep breaths that I mindfully exhaled. I began looking forward to the time spent alone in my vehicle. Occasionally I'd belt out a song at the top of my lungs, drumming to the tune on my steering wheel. Once, I forgot my window was down. Stopping at a red light mid-song, I happened to glance over at the driver in the next lane, and we both laughed.

If there's another secret to developing a mindful life, it could be in taking control of our time. Most of us are guilty of having said we "don't have time" for something, when in reality it is a matter of how we choose to spend the time we do have. While I've been known to lament a lack of time for exercise, I actually choose to write instead of exercise on my free mornings.

Laura Vanderkam compares our lives to a metaphorical garden in her book *Off the Clock*, suggesting that becoming our life's "master gardener" means deciding that you are responsible for how you spend your time and believing that much of time is a choice.

"But here's something we do all have: 24 hours in a day, 168 hours in a week. Whatever our constraints—our own or those that come from caring for others—by tending our gardens, we come closer, day by day, to building the lives we want in the time we've got," Vanderkam writes.

"Mindfulness gives you time. Time gives you choices. Choices lead to freedom, whatever one's plot of earth looks like," Vanderkam continues. "It is easy to fall into false narratives of time poverty, but choosing to change your story from 'I'm too busy' to 'I have time for what matters to me' can make you see possibilities. In time, such possibilities can make any garden bloom."

If we truly want to engage in an activity, to make time for it, something has to give, whether that is social engagements, television, Facebook, or other leisure (outside of employment) activities.

"Creating takes minutes and hours. Living a creative life means making room to dream, craft, compose, produce," Jen Hatmaker says in *Of Mess and Moxie*. "Art requires time, which, of course, you have none of. This is the creator's dilemma. You will not miraculously produce by carrying on exactly like you are. It's a whole thing, and you have to make room for it."

The bulk of this book was written on my days off. That meant keeping weekends open, missing events, and not socializing much on those open days—not too painful for someone who is an introvert by nature. In fact, on those days designated for writing, it wasn't unusual for me to not even get dressed until after noon, and I sometimes didn't leave the house at all over the weekend.

"When you carefully monitor your experience of time, then you don't mind if the time races by, not if you are immersed and engrossed and, after three hours, look down to discover seven pages of your novel completed. That is good speed. What you don't want is your life to speed by in the pursuit of nothing. Speed is not the issue; time is not the issue; the issue is the quality of your life. When you find yourself at home in your writing space, hush your mind, hold your dream, open to your work, and time will take care of itself. It may pass in slow motion, it may race by, or it may stop altogether: none of that is an issue, not if you are lost in the writing."

Eric Maisel's advice in *A Writer's Space* may have been aimed at authors, but it pertains to anyone wanting to live a more creative life. It's all about what we choose to do. If you need to schedule time in order to practice creativity, then write it on your calendar. I'd hazard a guess that most of us need to learn to breathe, to press pause and become mindful of our moments. With practice, mindfulness can become a habit.

"In a sense, we don't have time not to do mindfulness—it's that important. On the other hand, it's outside of time altogether. The present moment has very intense properties. The past is over, the future hasn't come yet, so there's only this moment," Jon Kabat-Zinn said in a Live Happy podcast for *Live Happy* magazine. "If you can learn how to live in this present moment, then mindfulness doesn't take any time at all. You're moving through life, surfing on your breath, and handling whatever comes up as you need to.

"And then, when you're doing it that way, instead of it being a drag . . . it can become a love affair with your life while you still have it to live."

When that happens, our life *becomes* the meditation.

Get out your crayons or colored pencils. In 2015, an estimated 12 million adult coloring books were sold in the United States, according to Nielsen Bookscan. There's a reason adult coloring books have become all the rage. Coloring pages can serve as a mindfulness technique, slowing heart rate and respiration, loosening muscles, and stimulating the brain. Coloring has the therapeutic potential to reduce anxiety and create focus. A 2017 study in the journal *Art Therapy* found the act of coloring an image lowered anxiety and improved mood. Alone, or in a group, take time out of your busy day to color one of these coloring pages. Put on some relaxing music, get a cup of tea or a glass of wine, and spend time just being as you color. For a short period of time, empty your mind of all your worries. Don't hurry through this activity. It is meant to be a time of slowing down and relaxation.

Creative Spark:
TWILA BELK

I met Twila Belk, also known as the "Gotta Tell Somebody Gal," in the summer of 2015, when she was a keynote speaker at the Cedar Falls Christian Writers Workshop. I was engaged by Twila's easygoing speaking style as well as the roster of books she'd either written or contributed to, including her recently released *Raindrops from Heaven: Gentle Reminders of God's Power, Presence, and Purpose.*

It soon became apparent how Twila had earned the Gotta Tell Somebody moniker: she loved bragging on God. We shared a special moment the last day of the conference, praying together and sharing concerns that lay heavy on our hearts. I was impressed by the bigness of her faith and her positive attitude in the face of challenges that included caring for a husband with disabilities.

"I had no idea that the words I wrestled with and cried out to God for as I wrote the daily readings for *Raindrops from Heaven* would end up ministering to me," Twila says.

In March 2016, Twila was diagnosed with triple negative breast cancer, an aggressive and recurrent form. She underwent chemotherapy and a bilateral mastectomy. It was during this time the readings in the devotional seemed to speak directly to her.

"I think God wanted me to write the book for me," Twila says. "That makes me smile."

During her treatment, the devotional's success led to her publisher's request for another book. Twila began writing *The Power to Be: Be Still, Be Grateful, Be Strong, Be Courageous* while she was still in treatment. The forty-day devotional has three recurring messages: knowing God, trusting God, and keeping attention on the right things.

"My job is to trust God with all my heart and acknowledge Him in all my ways," Twila says. "When I do that, He keeps His promise to take care of me, to make my path straight. I'm not left to flounder on my own. I've learned that I have no control over circumstances and that my circumstances don't change who God is; they show me who God is. I've had to let go of any control I thought I had and trust God."

Twila has experienced many adventures in her life. It isn't every woman who can claim status as a childhood entrepreneur. She sold painted rocks door to door, vegetables from her mom's garden, furry little creatures she made, and even pots and pans from her front porch.

During high school, Twila was an exchange student in Ecuador, and a few years later, in her early twenties, she became a certified journeyman machinist. Later portfolio credits include medical transcribing, directing writing conferences, working as a virtual assistant for acclaimed Christian writer Cecil Murphey, and co-owning a Christian bookstore and vending company with her husband, Steve.

"Steve and I hosted fun parties and invited the community to join us," Twila says about the days they operated the bookstore. "I wrote crazy, memorable radio ads and my husband and I voiced them. We had lots of fun."

The couple have also faced many trials in their forty years together, not the least of which is Steve's deteriorating health.

"I'm the primary provider now," Twila says. "Caring for my husband and all my other responsibilities takes up so much of my time, I'm not able to work as much. I've had to give up speaking and teaching and the book sales that come with those events. Bills continue to mount, and income continues to decrease. I grieve over what I've had to let go of."

Then she switches gears.

"But it is what it is right now. There are lots of things I don't understand. Proverbs 3:5–6 reminds me that I don't have to understand everything. In fact, I'm not supposed to. God and I have lots of talks, and He continues to assure me and carry me in His embrace of grace. A big lesson: Whatever I focus on becomes magnified. If I keep my attention on my challenges, they become overwhelming to me and tend to control my life. But if I fix my thoughts on God, He becomes magnified in my heart and mind. I'm reminded of who He is and what He's able to do. Having a grateful heart is key."

It's that grateful heart that sees God's blessings, even during the toughest times.

"God is so good to send me sweet surprises at just the right times. He proves again and again that He is my provider. One thing I've learned: God excels in impossible situations. I have so many God stories to tell."

She continues to do just that; after all, she's the Gotta Tell Somebody Gal.

"Gratitude is waking up each day, looking to the heavens from which all good things have their beginnings, sliding out of bed into the solid reality of another day, and grasping still another opportunity begging to be taken. The day is a thank you yet to be known, born out of imagination and ambition held close to our heart's desire."

—LEN FROYEN,
GRATITUDE: AFFIRMING ONE ANOTHER THROUGH STORIES

Chapter 8:
GRATITUDE ADJUSTMENT

◆

Our dreams are not always possible and tomorrow doesn't promise anything, but we can thank God for what we have today.

The more we thank God for every blessing, the more blessings we will see we can be thankful for!

◆

Please. Thank you. Excuse me. My parents raised their children to have good manners, and I've retained the habit, sometimes to the point of being excruciatingly polite. I was the woman in labor who apologized to the nurses and doctor for her cries of pain, or to cashiers when they made a mistake, as if I were the one at fault. I've even been known to apologize to a doorway when I bumped into it. So perhaps it was not so out of character when, two days after my husband's death, I picked up a journal and wrote down all the things I was thankful for:

- A life insurance policy that had been reinstated just twenty-seven days before.

- The five-and-a-half years I'd cherished with David since his cancer treatment, a period when our marriage was the best it had ever been.

- Recent conversations I'd had with my husband about what he'd want me to do if he died before me, a topic we hadn't seriously discussed before that, not even during his cancer.

- My daughter Emily having followed her compulsion in the three months previous to her dad's death to hug him and proclaim her love repeatedly each day.

- Siblings who rushed to my side when they heard the news.

The tally went on for three pages. No one told me to do this. They wouldn't have dared to suggest I compile a gratitude list less than forty-eight hours after a devastating loss. As a Christian, however, I'd vaguely recalled a Bible verse about "giving thanks in all things," and as a writer, journaling seemed the appropriate method of working through my grief. While it would seem a stretch so soon after his death, coming up with that long list of things I was grateful for was surprisingly easy. I've turned to those pages in my journal many times in the ensuing years, whenever I need a reminder that God did indeed go before me, preparing me to lose my husband.

Continual prayer was the one form of meditation that came naturally as grief propelled me into a running conversation with God. As I carefully considered, reflected, pondered, and *meditated* on those things that were true, just, pure, lovely, virtuous, or praiseworthy (from Philippians 4:8), I couldn't help but feel a semblance of gratitude.

"Gratitude is many things to many people," Sonja Lyubomirsky wrote in *The How of Happiness*. "It is wondering; it is appreciation; it is looking at the bright side of a setback; it is fathoming abundance; it is thanking someone in your life; it is thanking God; it is 'counting blessings.' It is savoring; it is not taking things for granted; it is coping; it is present-oriented."

According to Amy Morin in an article on PsychologyToday. com, multiple studies affirm that developing a sense of gratitude strengthens the ability to bounce back after trauma. She mentions a 2003 study in the *Journal of Personality and Social Psychology*, which found that gratitude was a major contributor to an individual's resilience following the September 11 terrorist attacks, and a 2006 study published in *Behavior Research and Therapy*, which suggests that Vietnam War veterans with higher levels of gratitude were less likely to experience posttraumatic stress disorder.

The study of gratitude as a science is a fairly recent phenomenon. Until the late 1990s, the topic had remained mostly within the realm of religious leaders and philosophers. That changed in October 2000, when the Templeton Foundation brought a group of thirteen scientists to Dallas, Texas, for the purpose of advancing the science of gratitude. They explored the subject from the perspectives of anthropology, biology, moral philosophy, psychology, and theology, drawing on their own research and examining the evidence that "an attitude of gratitude creates blessings."

In his book, *Thanks! How the New Science of Gratitude Can Make You Happier*, Dr. Robert Emmons, a professor of psychology at the University of California, Davis, details many of those blessings, including a strengthened immune system, lowered blood pressure, higher levels of positive emotions, more joy, and increased optimism and self-esteem. Emmons, who was present at that original Temple Foundation meeting, is considered one of the foremost authorities on the topic of gratitude in North America. He looks at gratitude as "receiving and accepting all of life as a gift."

"Without gratitude, life can be lonely, depressing and impoverished," Emmons says. "Gratitude enriches human life. It elevates, energizes, inspires, and transforms. People are moved, opened, and humbled through expressions of gratitude."

His definition of gratitude has two components. The first is an affirmation of goodness: affirming there are good things in the world, gifts and benefits we have received. This doesn't mean ignoring the complaints and burdens we carry, but looking at life as a whole and identifying some amount of goodness in our life. The second part is figuring out where that goodness comes from, acknowledging that it is outside of ourselves.

For me, that is part and parcel of faith: affirming that life is a gift and that goodness comes not because of something we do but from grace. My ability to see the good in circumstances likely derives from the humbling experience of having had goodness bestowed upon me by others during David's cancer and after his death.

Dr. Emmons views gratitude as a choice. Pete Sulack, America's leading stress reduction expert and founder of StressRX, agrees.

"'Negativity bias' is our brain's natural home base," Sulack said in a 2016 article featured on DailyPositive.com. "It's our go-to response in a stressful world. We tend to remember the bad while forgetting the good.

"Now we must learn a new way of seeing the world and interacting with it if we are to become resilient to the stress of living in a post-modern world," he continues before explaining that our brain is *neuroplastic*, with the ability to rewire itself by practicing a habit repeatedly—in this case, the habit of gratitude.

"It is a choice to look around and take in the beauty that surrounds us instead of seeing the ugly. It's a choice to remember the good and let go of the bad. It's a conscious decision to find things for which to be grateful each and every day. It's difficult, but it's worth it."

Choosing thankfulness under all sorts of circumstances isn't always easy, but it's a practice well worth cultivating for a more creative and innovative life.

"When we are stressed, we revert to behaviors that are routine, time-tested, and familiar—our 'go to' plan of action," Sulack is quoted in an Inc.com article written by Kate L. Harrison. "We do this because we are in survival mode. When we are stressed, we are using an industrial, assembly-line type of thinking, instead of creative, out-of-the-box thinking."

As we've touched on in previous chapters, that assembly-line mindset is counterproductive to creativity. According to Sulack, cultivating gratefulness as a habit can change that type of thinking.

"To be creative and get beyond those compensatory behaviors and try new ones, we must address the stress response," he says. "Gratitude is one powerful way to do that. When you are grateful, your stress is reduced and you experience positive emotions. These in turn help you remember peripheral details more vividly, think outside the box, and recognize common themes among random or unassociated ideas. All of this adds up to a more creative response."

A grateful attitude doesn't happen overnight. We can't just tell ourselves to look on the bright side. It's a process we need to practice and develop as a habit, training our mind to replace negative thoughts with positive ones. One way to do that is to reflect on a time in your life when you faced adversity and then consider good things that happened because of it. My husband did this naturally after his cancer. After suffering through six months of grueling treatment, he'd often take my hand in his and remark, "If it took cancer to get this kind of relationship, then I'm glad for the cancer."

I can look back and see how losing three important people in my life in the space of three years changed me in positive ways. I'm more empathetic, open, and eager to help others. I became a certified grief counselor and founded an annual grief retreat because of my loss, not in spite of it. I have intimately seen how God can bring good from bad.

"When times are tough, you can always be grateful for the push adversity gives you to learn and grow," Sulack explains. "While it is easy to take the path of least resistance, griping and complaining about your situation, true leaders know that pain is part of life, but suffering is optional. Choose gratitude. Choose joy. This will make you more creative and innovative—and ultimately more successful in any endeavor."

Blogger and author Sara Frankl did this. She knew her rare autoimmune disease was terminal, but she didn't let that stop her from living. In the face of immeasurable pain and despite her dire circumstances, Sara made a daily decision to choose joy. Her book *Choose Joy: Finding Hope and Purpose When Life Hurts*, demonstrates how that conscious decision resulted in a life of beauty and faith.

"I am blessed because I take nothing for granted. I love what I have instead of yearning for what I lack. I choose to be happy, and I am. It really is that simple," she wrote shortly before her death at age thirty-eight.

Gratitude isn't just for the good times. It can help us through the bad ones. The word derives from the Latin *gratia*, meaning grace or graciousness. Through grace, I can look back at a husband's bout with cancer and be grateful for a renewed marriage relationship that lasted another five-and-a-half years. Grace can mean falling to your knees at the side of the bed after experiencing the death of a loved one to thank God for bringing them into your life in the first place—the father who died when I was pregnant with my third child, the mother I had for an additional twenty-five years, the husband who unexpectedly died the day before his sixty-first birthday, and the eight-year-old grandson who went Home shortly after. It means filling three journal pages with thankfulness forty-eight hours after the death of a husband.

"You have to decide you want to be joyful," Thomas Kinkade writes in *Lightposts for Living*. "You have to trust that life, despite its ups and downs, is essentially wonderful, that the finished tapestry of your days will be a thing of beauty."

In pursuing our passions, following our hearts, and believing that life, and the people in the world, are mostly good, choosing gratitude and joy becomes second nature to us.

"If we are involved in doing what we were put on Earth to do, a joyful heart is almost guaranteed—even in the midst of deepest difficulties," Kinkade continues. "Consistent and durable joy is generated when we pursue a passion that is strong enough to carry us past pain, something so meaningful and absorbing that we can ignore unhappy circumstances."

Kinkade suggests another way of cultivating gratitude is through developing a servant's heart in acts of everyday service to others.

"You'll begin to realize the rewards that come from blessing others—the smile of appreciation from people at work, the thanks from the homeless person, the joy and enthusiasm of your children, the sigh of pleasure from your spouse as you rub his or her neck."

I can pinpoint when a real shift occurred in my relationship with David. Bogged down with bills and babies, by 2004 I'd lost sight of our marriage, to the point that during our twenty-fifth wedding anniversary party, I wondered if ours was even a marriage to be celebrated. But two years later, when David was diagnosed with a cancer that had a 50 percent survival rate, I was shocked into awareness of how much he meant to me. Faced with the prospect of losing him, I made the conscious decision to put my husband first, before house and children.

One day, after a long morning of radiation and chemotherapy, David collapsed on the couch in exhaustion. I knelt down in front of him. Gently removing his socks and shoes, I began rubbing his feet. In twenty-seven years of marriage, I'd never touched that man's feet. I looked up, and there were tears in David's eyes. From that pivotal moment, our relationship changed dramatically. We became true partners in a newly revitalized marriage. From back rubs to bringing cups of coffee to putting the other's needs in front of our own, we actively searched for opportunities to serve the other. Now, when I fold my teen's laundry or make a cup of tea for one of my daughters, I'm doing the same thing: serving with a servant's heart.

Here's the kicker in all of this: Not only does gratitude enhance your creative life—it enhances *you*. Grateful people are more apt to live a life of reaching out to others. Numerous studies corroborate this. Scientists at the Greater Good Science Center at the University of California, Berkeley, have studied the psychology, sociology, and neuroscience of well-being, finding that people who make gratitude a consistent part of their life are more likely to act with generosity and compassion.

It makes sense that humans are not only meant to be creative but to be generous as well. According to a report commissioned by the John Templeton Foundation, research suggests there is a propensity for generosity deep within us. In an overview of more than 350 studies published between 1971 and 2017, there seems to be ample evidence that humans are biologically wired for generosity. Prosocial behaviors that benefit others trigger our brains to produce endorphins, the feel-good hormone. Not only does it feel good, but helping people helps us.

"Giving social support—whether time, effort, or goods—is associated with better overall health in older adults and volunteering is associated with delayed mortality," a May 2018 John Templeton Foundation white paper states. "Generosity appears to have especially strong associations with psychological health and well-being."

In a study at the University of Zurich, researchers conducted an experiment using functional magnetic resonance imaging (fMRI) to understand how acts of generosity related to happiness. Their research revealed a "warm glow" from neural changes in the brain associated with happiness after any act of generosity, even the smallest act of kindness. In other words, practicing gratitude can make someone a *better* person.

Look at it this way: When we think of creativity, we automatically think of "making" or "creating" *something*. But consider for a moment how it could be in "making something" *of our lives* and, through the power of kindness, creating a kinder, gentler world.

Who would have thought kindness could be so powerful? A lot of people, actually. A quick Amazon search reveals over 7,000 books on the topic. Google the phrase "random acts of kindness" or the word "kindness," and it's evident an entire movement on the virtue has evolved. The globally recognized World Kindness Day is celebrated every November, and the Random Acts of Kindness (RAK) Foundation has extended that concept to a Random Acts of Kindness week in February. You can find an entire website, KindnessRocks.com, devoted to leaving painted stones in unexpected places to brighten people's days, a practice that has spread all over the world. And then there's the World Gratitude Map, a crowdsourcing project with the mission to share gratitude.

"It is moving your mind over to this place where I think we should all be, which is to keep our eyes on all that is good, beautiful, and possible in the world," Jacqueline Lewis, one of the project's creators, said in a 2013 LiveScience article on the gratitude project. Lewis, a writer with an interest in human resilience, has a vested interest in the project. When her mother, Joan Zawoiski Lewis, was diagnosed with pancreatic cancer, all she asked was that people do good deeds in her name. Her spirits were lifted by the reports of family and friends throughout the world doing just that. Jacqueline was certain that kept her mother alive for nearly twenty months longer than expected.

"While dying, her focus on these good deeds done by others kept her alive with end-stage pancreatic cancer past all reasonable prognosis," Jacqueline said. "The [World Gratitude Map] gives the rest of us a chance to move our eyes in the same direction, perhaps derive the same benefit."

My daughter Elizabeth and I weren't aware of any of this when we designed Random Acts of Kindness cards after my grandson Jacob died. All we knew was that his life had been much too short and we were determined his death would have meaning. He'd spent a great deal of his time in the hospital during the nearly three years he'd battled cancer. A dedicated band of Child Life Committee volunteers at the University of Iowa Hospital visited his room, bringing toys and involving him in activities designed to entertain young patients. Jacob, who sorely missed his siblings while he and his mom were in the hospital, would save the cupcakes he made with the volunteers to share with siblings back home. He'd raid his own piggy bank to purchase gifts for his big sister Becca at the hospital gift shop. And during a brief period of remission, he collected toys to take to other children in the hospital. On his deathbed, when he heard his mother complain about stiffness from sleeping on the floor next to him, his thin arm reached out from underneath the blanket to rub her back.

The best way we could honor such a precious child was to be more like him, to become better people because of him. To be kinder. We designed cards that included his name and the Jacob's Ladder Facebook Page and began doing random acts of kindness in memory of Jacob. All over the country there were people following his cancer journey who vowed to do the same. Medical bills were paid off anonymously, groceries purchased for needy families, and acts of kindness shared on the Facebook page. Other acts were smaller: paying for the person in line behind them at a fast food place or bringing flowers to a coworker. My granddaughter Becca came up with the simple but brilliant ideas of putting a dollar bill in a baggie with one of the cards and taping it to a pop machine or leaving quarters by the vacuum cleaner at the car wash.

A Random Act of Kindness brought to you~in memory of Jacob Flesher, a boy who taught us the real meaning of love and compassion...
6-24-2005 to 8-19-2013

Jacob bravely battled cancer for nearly three years. After his death, the Hospice nurses brought balloons for the family to release. This photo, taken by his mother, shows one of those balloons. The clouds behind the balloon form the sign language symbol for "I love you."

Check out Jacob's Facebook page at www.facebook.com/pages/Jacobs-Ladder/ and consider doing your own random act of kindness in Jacob's name.

We relished seeing kindness done in Jacob's name all over the country. Doing them ourselves helped us in our grieving. To this day, no matter how bad my day is going, performing one small act of kindness in Jacob's name can brighten it.

If you're looking for the warm glow from acts of generosity or a way to reduce your stress level so you can be more creative, searching for things you can be thankful for in your life is a great place to start.

IGNITE

Whether you decide to do your own random acts of kindness or begin a gratitude journal or jar, there are several books listed in the resource section that will help you get started. For the purpose of this activity, however, spend time literally counting your blessings. What are you grateful for in your life? What life experiences have made you a better person? When did you see good come from bad?

Create a Gratitude List:

_____

_____

_____

_____

_____

_____

_____

_____

_____

_____

_____

_____

_____

_____

_____

_____

Creative Spark:
SUE BONEBRAKE

The first time I met Sue was in a barn full of animals. I'd arrived to interview her for a newspaper story on retirement and second careers. She and her husband, Sig, former high school teachers, were now in the business of raising alpacas.

Sue met Sig at Northwest Missouri State University where she was studying to be a teacher. They soon discovered they'd each had a poem published in the same copy of the *Lyrical Iowa* poetry anthology and that Sig's poem had been Sue's favorite. She took that as a sign. After a whirlwind romance that Sue recently chronicled in an essay published in *Chicken Soup for the Soul: The Miracle of Love,* they got married and had three children.

During their fifty years together, the two were always on the lookout for adventures. While they were still in college, they almost joined a national theater touring company, made plans to go into catfish farming, and briefly considered teaching on a reservation in Montana. When they lived in Sidney, Iowa, Sue worked as assistant director and did tech with a professional dinner theatre while Sig did tech and acted. Later, though both were teachers at the time, they did computer portraits and made homemade egg rolls on the NE Iowa fair circuit during summers. In 1991, Sue became director of a theater group that she ran for ten years. The two also taught English, speech, and drama at the high school I graduated from, Maquoketa Valley in Delhi, Iowa, for many years before their retirement.

"We were always up for adventure, doing things other people wouldn't even think of doing," Sue said, an understatement considering her husband had once been a trapeze artist.

The couple hadn't planned on becoming alpaca farmers when they visited an alpaca farm in 2003. Looking forward to retirement, they'd had a brand-new house built. They'd only wanted to see in person the domesticated species of South American camelid Sue had heard about on late-night television commercials. When a colleague told them of a farm nearby, they planned a one-hour visit. They stayed for seven hours. When the farmer drove the herd to the barn, there was no sound. It was that silence that won them over.

"In high school, when the bell rings, it's chaos—organized chaos, but it's always loud," Sue said. "When the herd of eighty alpacas ran past us on their way to the barn, there was no sound. I thought then that this would be heaven—you get out of a noisy school and there would be silence."

They purchased a male and two pregnant females, boarding them for eleven months before they sold their new house in town and moved to an acreage in Earlville, Iowa, where they now raise alpacas and Shetland sheep. It actually didn't surprise their children, who had grown up being involved in their parents' many adventures. They just shook their heads and murmured, "There they go again."

When Sue joined my lifelong learners group, it had been over fifty years since she'd had anything published. She hadn't stopped writing the poetry that had brought her and her husband together—she just hadn't submitted anything, the surest way to avoid rejection. But when she read one of her poems aloud, I was in awe of her obvious talent. With a little guidance and encouragement (and sometimes that's all it takes), she was off, polishing poetry and prose pulled from her file folders. Once she took that first step, she admitted she couldn't stop writing and submitting. It was as if a fire had been lit beneath her.

That fire continues to spread to other ventures in creativity. Though she has been taking painting lessons for five years, she recently began entering paintings in the county fair, as well as continuing with her photography, winning several blue ribbons in both categories.

"I don't plan on stopping either," Sue says. "Creative adventures keep life interesting."

---◆---

He tore me up into little pieces
   that fluttered to the ground.
As I bent to pick them up
   an overwhelming hurt filled me
And the pieces floated away
   in a flood of hot tears.
"Forget me." he said,
   and then turned around and walked away.
I stared at his retreating footsteps
   in the sand.
"No." I said, and it was only a whisper,
   but he heard;
He turned around and I could feel
   his eyes on me.
He sighed.
The soft worried sigh I knew so well.
And it floated past me in the breeze.
My eyes were drawn to his by an unseen force.
And then,
   before I could read what was written in them,
His back was to me and he was leaving again.
The heavy emptiness inside me
   kept me from following.
I gathered together all of me I could find—
      and went the other way.

MP —age 16

---◆---

Poetry is an art form I dabbled in as a teen but never perfected. I wrote this poem shortly after my first boyfriend broke up with me through a note inside my high school locker one morning. The discovery left me an emotional wreck for the remainder of the day; I skipped most of my classes to cry in the bathroom until the bus arrived to carry me back home. Normally, town students were taken to the elementary school, but on this particular day, the bus driver took an alternate route, dropping me off at the bottom of the gravel hill to our driveway. I'll never know for certain, but I suspect he couldn't bear to hear the sobs or see the puffy, red-rimmed eyes of the teenage girl crouched miserably in the front seat behind him.

Dad was outside working on a vehicle when he was startled by the unexpected bus stop. My heart sank when I saw him walking down the driveway to meet me. I would have preferred telling my mother, but there he stood, blocking my route to the house. There was no avoiding it—unless I pushed past him, I would have to explain the hurt I'd experienced to a man who'd never been comfortable with expressing emotion.

"Steve broke up with me," I managed to choke out as I thrust the crumpled, tear-stained note clutched in my hand toward him. Dad unfolded the paper and silently read it. I couldn't meet his eyes, fully expecting him to break out into a lyrical rendition of "Feelings."

"Feelings, nothing more than feelings," he'd often mock my moodiness with the first lines of Morris Albert's song. Instead, he surprised me by uncharacteristically reaching out to lift my chin, imparting some of the wisest advice I've ever gotten.

"I know it hurts and you can't see it right now, but there will be other boys. And if he broke up with you that way and can't see what a wonderful girl you are, then he didn't deserve you anyway."

When I so desperately needed understanding and compassion, my dad came through for me. I should have been penning poetry about a father's stoic devotion instead of pining for what I'd mistaken as lost love, but alas, I was only sixteen.

The English word "poem," or "poetry," came from the Greek word *poiema*, which is translated as "workmanship" in Ephesians 2:10

in the Bible: "For we are his workmanship, created in Christ Jesus for good works, which God prepared beforehand that we should walk in them." Essentially, we are God's poetry, his masterpiece.

While my writing certainly hasn't reached masterpiece level, it's evident I do have a history of writing my way through difficult periods of my life, beginning with teen angst then through my husband's cancer in 2006 to my mother's death in 2010. I'd assumed the reason I turned to journaling as I mourned my husband was because I was a writer. Weeks into my grief journey, however, I wondered how anyone could survive the experience *without* writing about it.

In an attempt to understand my own, I began researching the topic of grief as though studying for a final exam: reading dozens of books and articles about the grieving process. In doing so, I stumbled across repeated references to expressive writing as a healing tool.

While diary-keeping is nothing new, the therapeutic potential of reflective writing came into vogue in the 1960s, when Dr. Ira Progoff, a psychologist in New York, began offering intensive journaling workshops and classes. He'd been using a "psychological notebook" method in his therapy clients for several years before that. In the 1970s, he wrote several books, including *At a Journal Workshop*, detailing his intensive journal process. Around the same time, Christina Baldwin released her book *One to One: Self-Understanding through Journal Writing*, based on the adult education journal classes she taught.

But it is Dr. James Pennebaker who is often lauded as the pioneer in studying expressive writing as a route to healing. Pennebaker, Regents Centennial Chair of Psychology at the University of Texas in Austin, discusses his findings in his book *Opening Up: The Healing Power of Expressive Emotions*, revealing how short-term, focused writing can have a beneficial effect for anyone dealing with stress or trauma. In his original study in the late 1980s, college students wrote for fifteen minutes total on four consecutive days about the most traumatic or upsetting experiences of their lives, while control subjects were instructed to write about superficial topics. Those in the experimental group showed marked improvement in immune system functioning and had fewer visits to the health center in the months following the study. Not only that, but despite an occasional initial increase in distress during the first session of writing, there was a marked improvement in their emotional health.

In another one of Pennebaker's studies, fifty middle-aged professionals who were terminated from a large Dallas computer company were split into two groups. The first group wrote for thirty minutes a day, five days in a row, about their personal experience of being fired. The second group wrote for the same period of time on an unrelated topic. Within three months, 27 percent of the expressive writers had landed jobs compared with less than 5 percent of the participants in the control group.

Initially skeptical of Pennebaker's remarkable findings, Dr. Edward J. Murray, a professor of psychology at the University of Miami, conducted his own investigations, eventually agreeing that writing seems to produce therapeutic benefits that include health, cognitive, self-esteem, and behavior changes. "Writing seems to produce as much therapeutic benefit as sessions with a psychotherapist," he concluded.

Pennebaker's original expressive writing paradigm has been replicated in hundreds of studies, each measuring different potential effects of expressive writing. Not only has subsequent research confirmed his original findings regarding physical well-being, writing about emotionally charged topics has been shown to improve mental health, reducing symptoms of depression or anxiety. This has proven true in studies with those who have experienced loss, veterans experiencing PTSD, and HIV and cancer patients. Expressive writing now seems to be an accepted alternative holistic and non-medicinal form of therapy for emotional health.

Pennebaker's research did reveal that the type of writing mattered; there seemed little benefit to whining and venting without reflection. It was important to look for meaning in the experiences. He also discovered that healing writing didn't have to be trauma-focused; writing about happy experiences and positive thoughts and feelings was also associated with health benefits.

None of this requires writing talent. There's just something about putting pen to paper that is beneficial, whether it is journaling, blogging, or writing for publication. Even writing letters counts. In one study, Kent State professor Steven Toepfer discovered that having students write three letters a week, spending fifteen to twenty minutes on each letter, decreased depressive symptoms and increased happiness and life satisfaction significantly.

I experienced the letter-writing benefit after David's death. Because he'd died on a Tuesday, I began dreading Tuesdays, a weekly reminder of my loss. When I made the decision to reach out to someone else every Tuesday, through a card or handwritten letter, I began looking forward to Tuesdays. Writing letters to others ending up helping *me*.

While I have maintained throughout this book that being more creative means opening up your mind, trying new things, allowing yourself to fail, and finding ways to work creativity in your everyday life, expressive writing is the one craft I have specifically and consciously honed since I was a teen. That served me well when I turned to writing to get through situations much tougher than a doomed teenage romance. The ease with which I wrote articles, essays, and even an entire book (*Refined by Fire: A Journey of Grief and Grace*) about the loss of my husband caused me to wonder why I hadn't written more about Jacob, the grandson who died some seventeen months after his grandfather. It was as though I'd decided the loss was more my daughter's and her husband's, as the parents. I'd hesitated to claim it as my own.

Elizabeth had noticed. "You didn't write enough about Jacob," she'd lamented after reading *Refined by Fire*, and I'd replied that it was her story to tell. It wasn't until working on this book, nearly five years after his death, that I wrote a poem about Jacob. I'd been encouraging members of a writing group I facilitated to enter a poetry contest. In turn, they challenged me to do the same. I struggled to write a poem about rubbing the feet of those I loved; first my dad when I was a child, then my husband's during his cancer treatment, and, finally, my mother's while she lay dying on her deathbed.

I'd even chosen the title: "Love's Disciple." I wrote, revised, reword-
ed, and rewrote again. I was ready to give up on poetry altogether
when, almost as if it had a mind of its own, the words began flowing
seamlessly and a new poem formed. A lump formed in my throat
and tears stung my eyes. They were the same words I'd used in my
book, but they somehow carried more power in the abbreviated
poetry version.

Jacob I Have Loved
Tentatively, I approach
the small form hidden
beneath the blankets.
Standing silently,
I wait
straining to hear a breath,
to see the rise of a chest
expanded with vileness.
One small movement
reveals a thin arm
I reach out to touch,
skin hot and dry as paper.
I fall to my knees
in homage
of his holiness.
Head bowed close,
I whisper
"Tell your grandpa I miss him."

———— ◆ ————

I don't claim to be a poet; I have written perhaps a dozen poems
in my life, including the one I penned at age sixteen. It wasn't that
Jacob's poem was so well written, but something unexpected happened as I worked on it: I began sobbing, allowing myself to feel
the full weight of sorrow at losing such a beautiful boy. As if for the
first time, I claimed my loss and, in doing so, could begin healing.

I preach the therapeutic benefits of writing in my "Expressive Writing for Healing" workshops, but there is always the chance someone might think it works for me precisely because I am a writer by trade and that it is not applicable to them. But it was only through a form of writing I do *not* practice, poetry, that I experienced a mending of the gaping wound left by Jacob's death. Now I can say with some certainty, even if you are not a writer, as I am not a poet, expressive writing can be a valuable tool in our arsenal against despair, as well as a creative outlet. And, as with any creative outlet, it takes time to develop the habit of creating.

In *The Artist's Way*, author and creativity guru Julia Cameron claims a secret to productivity and getting rid of the clutter in your brain is to write every morning. "Morning Pages" practice means filling three blank pages of a notebook or journal with stream-of-consciousness writing first thing every day—a brain dump, so to speak.

"There is no wrong way to do Morning Pages," Cameron says on her website. "They are not high art. They are not even 'writing.' They are about anything and everything that crosses your mind—and they are for your eyes only."

Mark Levy calls it "freewriting" in his book *Accidental Genius: Using Writing to Generate Your Best Ideas, Insight, and Content.* In both cases, journaling and freewriting, the idea is to write as freely and as close to stream of consciousness as possible, freeing your mind so it can be more creative. That means no editing. At least not as long as the writing is for yourself. Eventually, you might want your writing to reach an audience through blogging or publication.

During my husband's cancer treatment in 2006, I wrote daily while he was in the hospital after his surgery. After he was released, I wrote sporadically throughout the week—but consistently on Wednesdays, during his chemotherapy treatments. I'd sit next to him, holding his hand with my free one while I wrote with the other. What I wrote during those months, about cancer, caregiving, and what was happening in our marriage relationship, eventually became a book chronicling a true love story of a relationship renewed by caregiving, *Chemo-Therapist: How Cancer Cured a Marriage.* After

David's death, my "housewife writer" blog morphed into a grieving one for a while. I still get emails from widows and widowers thanking me for those posts that guide them in their own grief journey. Pieces of that blog and my private journal appear in *Refined by Fire*.

As a writer, however, there are times when I have trouble beginning an essay, article, or chapter of a book, moments when writing grinds to a halt. My husband used to quip "The hardest part is getting started," and he was right. When I face those times, it helps to just sit down and begin writing, even if what I'm producing has little value and won't make it into the final piece. I call it "greasing the writing wheels." I might even begin a work session by writing a letter to a friend.

For writers, especially, it's important to keep those wheels greased, to incorporate writing as a daily activity. Gretchen Rubin addresses this in her book *The Happiness Project*.

"Step by step, you make your way forward. That's why practices such as daily writing exercise or keeping a daily blog can be so helpful. You see yourself do the work, which shows you that you can do the work. Progress is reassuring and inspiring; panic and despair set in when you find yourself getting nothing done day after day. One of the painful ironies of work life is that the anxiety of procrastination often makes people even less likely to buckle down in the future."

"Day by day, we build our lives, and day by day, we can take steps toward making real the magnificent creations of our imaginations," Rubin's wisdom continues in her follow-up book, *Happier at Home*.

If you are new to expressive writing and would like to get started on the practice, these are suggestions I share in my *Expressive Writing for Healing* book and workshops:

1. **Choose a notebook or journal that fits your personality, that you can comfortably write in.** A beautiful leather-bound journal might be too intimidating to begin with. Perhaps it will be one with a cover design that has special meaning to

you: a butterfly, a dragonfly, or a Bible verse. Or maybe you'd prefer a simple notebook with pages that can easily be torn out. Just the act of handwriting can be therapeutic, but if you're more comfortable typing on a computer, that's fine too. Choose whatever works for you and your lifestyle.

2. **There are no rules in journal writing.** Cross out sentences, scribble on the sides of the paper, doodle or draw on the pages. Don't worry about sentence structure or grammar. This writing is for you and not an audience. You can't help yourself if you're holding back, afraid to be honest about what you're feeling. Feelings and emotions can be messy, so it's perfectly fine if your journal is too.

3. **Write down your dreams, both literal and figurative.** What do you want your more creative life to look like? Do you have dreams and desires for your future? Write them down. In a couple of years, you may look back and see some have become reality. Our subconscious also works hard at processing significant changes in our life. Have you had any particularly vivid nighttime dreams? Write those down too. I've experienced several dreams about David where I could feel his arms around me or hear his voice. I woke up feeling as though he'd actually visited me. I've also solved daytime dilemmas and come up with wonderful ideas in my dreams, so I like to keep a notebook by the bed to jot them down. I know better than to think I'll remember in the morning.

4. **If you are reading inspirational books or articles, copy passages or quotes that speak to you.** When I read something particularly inspiring or uplifting that resonates with me, I transcribe pertinent passages or quotes in my journal. I often refer to those past journals and continue to find inspiration and encouragement from the words I copied down. That said, make sure the books and articles you read are bringing light to your soul. Just as our journal writing needs to focus

on finding meaning in a situation, so should our reading. Be a discerning reader. There are too many inspirational and encouraging books available to bother reading one that makes you feel worse.

5. **Date your journal entries, and end them on a positive note.** We've learned how important gratitude is to our happiness and creativity. Strive to find one thing to be grateful for each time you journal. By ending your journal entry on a positive note—with words of thanks or perhaps a prayer—you are training yourself to consciously choose joy and gratitude. This practice works because it forces you to intentionally focus your attention on grateful thinking, eliminating unwanted, ungrateful thoughts and guarding against taking things or people for granted. You want gratitude to become a habit, so practicing it in your journal helps that happen.

"We write, we make music, we draw pictures, because we are listening for meaning, feeling for healing," Madeleine L'Engle says in *Walking on Water*. "And during the writing of the story or the painting or the composing or singing or play, we are returned to that open creativity which was ours when we were children."

Writing, just like painting, drawing, music, or photography, could be the workmanship you are designed for. If nothing else, it can serve as a form of meditation or a tool in your arsenal to help heal from those inevitable hurts we all experience in this life. All you need is a pencil and a piece of paper to begin.

"Creativity is a safe zone,
and there is no place for
self-judgement. While your
mind might pipe in now and
then, remind yourself that art is
a path toward nurturing your
self-expression and your
happiest self."

—REBECCA SCHWEIGER

Think you aren't a writer? That you can't benefit from creative or expressive writing? Think again! You don't have to be a writer to pen your way through a tough time, just as you don't have to be a poet to enjoy playing with words. You don't even have to write the words yourself.

Let's try blackout poetry. Turn out the lights and grab a flashlight. No, not really. Blackout poetry focuses on circling and arranging words that are already there on a page of previously published words, such as the page of a newspaper or book. Commonly attributed to author Austin Kleon, the practice entails using a permanent marker to cross out or eliminate words, keeping those words you choose. Kleon hit on the technique as a way of overcoming writer's block, working with copies of *The New York Times*. His resulting blackout poems posted on his blog led to the release of his first book, *Newspaper Blackout*. Search the following page of text, emphasizing chosen words by blacking out the ones around them. It's not necessary to read the page before you cross out words since the idea is to create a new work. Your resulting poem can be read from left to right or top to bottom.

You can find examples of blackout poems on Austin Kleon's Newspaper Blackout website, https://newspaperblackout.com.

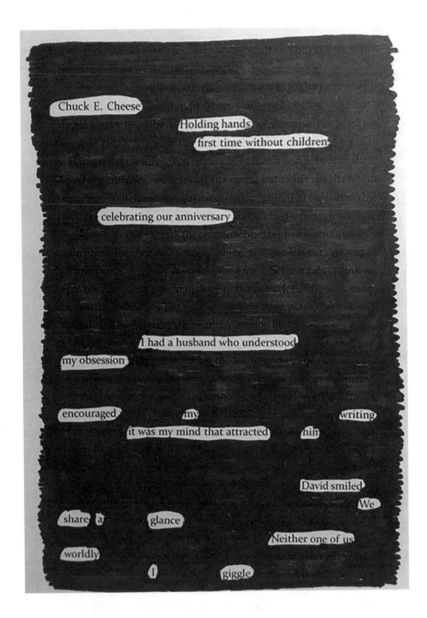

Chuck E. Cheese
Holding hands
first time without children

celebrating our anniversary

I had a husband who understood
my obsession

encouraged   my   writing
it was my mind that attracted   him

David smiled
We
share a   glance
Neither one of us
worldly
I   giggle

Mary's first attempt at blackout poetry.

Use these two pages for your own blackout poetry.

What was it about couponing and refunding that appealed to me, and not to others? What got me started in this incredibly rewarding hobby? Certainly my mother had used a few coupons but never to any great extent. For one thing, she and my father could barely afford the newspapers or magazines that carried the coupons. As parents raising ten children on a low income, they struggled just to put food on the table and clothes on our backs. My father raised chickens for their eggs and meat and planted and tended a huge garden every year. My mother canned or froze their abundant harvest, sewed many of our clothes, made our dolls, braided rag rugs, and gutted the chickens that became a staple of our Sunday dinners.

If using coupons was simply a matter of saving money and the product of a person's upbringing, then one would presume that most of my siblings, also raised in poverty, would be avid cou-poners as well. While they are frugal and shop thrift stores, of the ten of us, I was the only one that could be described as a coupon enthusiast until one sister joined me in the hobby last year.

Was it something innate in my personality then that attracted me to couponing and refunding? As a child I had the makings of a future coupon queen, dissipated my fears. But on the night my mother passed away, my long-held fear of dying ceased. Perhaps it was the way she'd faced death or her anticipation to be with my father. Maybe it was watching my siblings gently care for her as she lay peacefully dying. After a lifetime struggle to impart her faith to her children, through her death, my mother had somehow managed to leave me a legacy of faith.

My mother had been a consummate artist and a highly creative woman. Having lived in poverty for most of her life, she didn't have much in the way of material things. When it came time for my siblings and me to divide up her possessions, it was her art we coveted—the paintings, wood carvings, and handmade teddy bears. As the writer in the family, I became the "keeper of her words," inheriting many of her notebooks and several unpublished manuscripts. I also had a thick memory book she'd filled out for me. During the months following her death, I read and reread her writing. With my husband's blessing, I also spent many hours alone in her empty house that winter, working on a book. David encouraged my lone writing sessions, hugging me goodbye at the door and handing me a travel mug of hot tea he'd made me for the road.

During breaks from the intensity of writing, I'd push my chair back from my mother's vintage oak

Creative Spark:
SHELLY BEACH

Shelly Beach captured my attention the minute she opened her mouth to present at a writer's conference I attended in June 2011. A powerful speaker, she is a dynamo, with more than ten published books to her name, extensive editing credentials, and a prison ministry. Shelly personifies my audience for this book. Her initial reaction when she heard the topic was, "Oh, I'm not really creative."

"I wasn't raised in a home where creativity was encouraged," Shelly continued before pausing to reflect on what she'd just said.

"But my mother was creative, in her own way," Shelly added. "She couldn't paint a picture, knit, sew, or write creatively. But she could entertain children for hours and hold them spellbound with stories. She gave the perfect gift you never knew you wanted until you lifted the lid or peeled back the paper. In an era when missionary wives were gifted with Tupperware and tea towels, my mother bought them eyebrow-raising lingerie. She believed they should be gifted with special extravagances that helped them feel beautiful and that women love."

Despite a lack of encouragement, a young Shelly still practiced a wide variety of creative endeavors.

"I sang, played a variety of instruments, joined a band, and even wrote a few songs. I also wrote poetry and stories and was hired to write for a local newspaper," Shelly says. "I began submitting and publishing successfully with magazines, but I still never considered myself a 'real writer' until someone else urged me to claim my calling. I'll never forget the first time a writer I respected—an author and speaker named Sandra—called me a writer. I was attending a conference, and Sandra had just read a sample of my work. She looked into my eyes and said, 'Shelly, *you are* a writer, so start calling yourself one.' Her words both elated me and terrified me. I'd always wanted to be a writer, and although I'd published articles and short stories, I didn't consider myself a *real* writer like Sandra. I didn't believe I was creative enough or as good as everyone else."

Like so many of us, Shelly struggled to see herself the way others saw her, to claim the creative self God designed her to be.

"Sandra made a pathway in the wilderness for me to see the creative gifts God had given me. His limitless creativity is woven into each of us as His image-bearers," Shelly acknowledges. "I was born creative. God gave me talents, abilities, and a passion for writing, and it's my job to use my gifts to create meaning and beauty that reflects His beauty in the world."

Shelly's life has not been without challenges. She experienced both a childhood sexual assault and an encounter with a serial rapist when she was just nineteen. Her writing grew out of personal experience. She was married and the mother of two when she became critically ill in 1999. She'd been experiencing dizziness, headaches, and other neurological symptoms for over a year when her condition deteriorated rapidly. Within days, she was unable to stand or walk, her vision went double, and she was vomiting relentlessly. Doctors believed she had a glioblastoma, an aggressive form of brain cancer, but that was soon ruled out and she was treated with steroids and released from the hospital. For the next sixteen years she lived with mild symptoms of multiple sclerosis (MS) but remained active, traveling, speaking, and writing.

In late 2014, Shelly experienced tingling in her face. Neuro evaluations revealed a second lesion on her brain stem. She underwent brain surgery followed by sixteen months of illness and confusion as doctors disagreed about what she was dealing with. In the spring of 2015, Shelly was diagnosed with relapsing-remitting MS with lesions that present primarily in the brain stem. While her pace has slowed due to symptoms that include fatigue, pain, headaches, and weakened walking, Shelly continues to write, speak, mentor, and edit.

"God has gifted me with the opportunity to create beauty and meaning from my life experiences. We're all given precious opportunities to birth something new from the mess of our lives in ways that give hope to others. This is my passion in writing and creating."

Chapter 10:
TRIBAL ART

◆

In my 30's I joined the Dubuque Art Association that held shows and had meetings in the Public Library. It was only a block away and Bud would watch the children while I learned more about Art once or twice a month. The Library was also a source of Art information, so many books to enjoy. Bud also liked to read and so did the children.

◆

"You only need one friend," my mother once told me. At the time, in fourth or fifth grade, I would have been thrilled to have a single friend. Instead, I was the class pariah; a shy, poor girl whose motley secondhand wardrobe smelled of cigarette and wood smoke. I was always chosen last for teams, and no one played with me at recess. I endured name-calling, shoves against the wall, and being tripped in the hallway. I was even spit at on occasion. I learned to navigate the school hallways with my books clutched tightly to my chest, shoulders hunched, eyes always cast downward so as not to meet those of potential tormentors. I have no fond memories of elementary school. It was there I learned to distrust females with sporadic offers of friendship that were hastily withdrawn when the meanest girl in school subsequently aimed her wrath at them.

Ironically, while my parents struggled mightily to send their children to parochial school, it wasn't until entering public school in seventh grade that I escaped the bowels of my own private hell and made some of my first real friends.

Thanks to a babysitting job that allowed for a few new clothing purchases and several excellent teachers who encouraged my natural talents, I gained enough confidence to join clubs and participate in after-school activities. I wrote for the newspaper, participated in speech and drama, and even played the lead in several high school plays. These experiences brought me situational friendships, at least: girls who were involved in the same activities, but we lost touch after high school. As an adult, outside of a husband who was my best friend, my six sisters, and some pen pal relationships, I'd managed to cultivate but a single friendship.

Mary Humston and I met in Iowa City in 1986, when David and I moved there so he could pursue an MA in social work. Mary had three children, and I was pregnant with my third. We were both stay-at-home moms with writing aspirations and a coupon hobby. Mary introduced me to a mother's playgroup, La Leche League, and *Mothering* magazine, exposing me to a wide array of mothering styles, including the attachment parenting and homeschooling I would later embrace as my own. While David's degree was abandoned when we moved away the following year, my friendship with Mary was not. For the next thirty years, she and I would share a relationship we'd later chronicle in *Mary & Me: A Lasting Link Through Ink*, a book about a friendship linked by thousands of letters. I believed my mother was right: one friendship was enough. I had a husband who was my best friend. I had sisters. And then there was Mary. I was too busy raising eight children to cultivate or maintain other close relationships.

It wasn't until June 2011, after reading my deceased mother's notebooks and seeing her repeated admonition to utilize one's talents, that I decided I'd honor Mom by taking my writing seriously and attending my first writer's conference. Thanks to the encouragement of a supportive spouse, I signed up for the Christian Writers Workshop in Cedar Falls, Iowa.

I don't know how long I stood in front of the closed door of the conference center when I arrived, steeling myself for whatever kind of judgement lay on the other side. I was a fifty-one-year-old woman with a fairly successful writing résumé, but it was Raggedy Mary who hesitated to open it and step inside.

"She haunts me sometimes, the raggedy girl. Mismatched socks, ratty hair, a skinny body averse to baths," Mary DeMuth writes in her memoir *Thin Places*. A "raggedy girl" who was bullied mercilessly as a child remains inside me as well. Yet it had been my raggedy roots that had driven me to write in the first place, to succeed at something. To prove, as DeMuth writes, "I am worthy to take up space on this earth." Writing gave me the voice I never had as a bullied child.

I didn't expect the warm welcome I got at the conference or the feeling of camaraderie I experienced in a room full of people interested in the same thing. I walked into a room filled with strangers the first day of that workshop. Three days later, I left with something I hadn't managed to obtain in the previous thirty years: several fledgling female friendships.

When David died nine months later, a group of those women showed up at his wake, and I began to see the benefits of having more than one good friend. Yes, my sisters and Mary Humston proved to be a loyal support system for me in the months following David's death. Mary traveled once a month for eighteen months to take me out to lunch and ask the questions no one else dared ask. Her frequent letters continued to serve as a lifeline. But because I had forged other friendships, I also had Sue and Jean, who sent cards of encouragement. Wanda, Kristi, Robyn: all friendships formed at that initial writers workshop. Then seventeen months after my husband's death, there was Mona, who, intimately knowing the loss of a grandchild, appeared on my doorstep in her pajamas on the morning of my grandson's wake. For the first time in my adult life, my heart was open to friendship, and I've made many more cherished friends as a result.

"But for the most part, there are friends who are forever part of you and your journey. Those you can cry with, sharing griefs and faults. Those you can laugh with, free and joyful as small children in uninhibited mirth," Madeleine L'Engle writes in *Friends for the Journey*. "Those who have proven time and again that they can be counted on. Those you can pray with on the deepest level, exposing yourselves totally to God's love. I have been richly blessed by such friends, and for each of them I daily give deep thanks. Yes, friendship is risky. But the risk is worth it. It is worth it to strip off your protective coating. To be vulnerable. To be known. To risk being loved."

I discovered the value of friends as a support system during tough times, but it turns out that friendships are also good for our health. When Julianne Holt-Lunstad, professor of psychology at Brigham Young University, did a meta-analysis of 148 studies, she concluded that a lack of social support increased the risk of premature death by 50 percent, an effect on mortality risk comparable to smoking up to fifteen cigarettes a day.

The root of the Hebrew word for friendship, *chaver*, is the word *chibur*, meaning "connection." Feeling connected to others contributes to better health, improved immunity, and a reduced risk of heart disease and depression. In fact, in a Harvard longitude study of nearly three hundred men over the course of seventy-five years, having meaningful relationships was identified as the only thing that truly matters in life.

Robert Waldinger, MD, the director of the Harvard study, was quoted in an *AARP* magazine interview as saying the quality of your relationships at age fifty is a better predictor of your future health than your cholesterol levels. How many friends are needed to see that kind of benefit? Not as many as you'd think.

"The research doesn't show you have to have a ton of friends and love cocktail parties," Waldinger said. "It just means you have some close connections. It could be one. It could be two."

Technically, then, my mother had been correct: we do only need one friend. Unfortunately, some people don't even have that. According to a "girlfriend" survey conducted by *Family Circle* magazine, 4 percent of respondents reported having no friends at all. The majority, 52 percent, said they had between three and five friends, and only 19 percent had six or more.

There appears to be a whole lot more Raggedy Marys out there. A full 17 percent reported a lack of confidence as the reason for not establishing more friendships, and 5 percent cited a history of being rejected as preventing them from even trying to establish friendships.

Considering our increasingly busy lives, the greatest barrier to establishing friendships should be no surprise: 40 percent of respondents said a lack of time was their single greatest obstacle to making friends as an adult.

Friendships do take time to cultivate and nurture—36 percent of those surveyed got together with friends one or more times a week, one in four texted a friend daily, and one in five touched base via social media four or more times a day. Those things are hard to prioritize in our lives when we have children, jobs, and maybe aging parents to contend with. Yet to look at some of our social media statistics, it appears as though we have plenty of friends.

Considering I had few real friends until seven years ago, how on Earth did I manage to accumulate 550 on Facebook? Several of my Facebook "friends" claim over 1000 relationships. Despite those kinds of numbers on social media, research demonstrates we can't possibly maintain that number of close relationships. In fact, according to anthropologist Robin Dunbar, the average number of friendships a person can maintain is about 150.

"It's the number of people you know as persons and you know how they fit into your social world and they know how you fit in theirs. They are a group of people to which you have an obligation of friendship," Dunbar says.

Dunbar's number, 150, refers to those people with whom you have a personalized relationship, one that is based around general obligations of trust and reciprocity. The circle of 150 consists of four layers called circles of acquaintanceship: an inner circle of 5 core people, then successive layers of 15, 50, and 150. With each successive circle, the number of people in it increases but the emotional intimacy decreases. That inner core includes those people you might consider calling in the middle of the night if you needed them.

At that first writers' conference, I connected with women and men who shared my interests in writing and being published. Later, I would make additional friends outside of that Christian writers' circle through a workplace setting, classes I taught, and my involvement in grief ministry. The first "tribe" I formed was a Bible study I held at church for two years before moving it into my home: a group of people with the common desire to connect with God. The initial group at the church included fifty participants. Five years later, seven of us continued to meet. The lifelong learners group at my library was the second of my own making, an attempt to gather like-minded individuals who wanted to imbibe in creative endeavors. When I began working at a spirituality center in mid-2018, I immediately began a similar "Artisans Soul" club and formed a "Faith Writers" group, all in the name of finding my tribe, choosing to spend time with people I wanted to be more like.

It was entrepreneur and motivational speaker Jim Rohn who said, "You are the average of the five people you spend the most time with." That could be good news, or sobering, depending on who those five people are for you. While we might not have much control over who we work with, when it comes to friends, it means we should be choosing carefully.

The Longevity Project, which studied over a thousand people from youth to death, found that the groups you associate with often determine the type of person you become. In *The Start-up of You*, Reid Hoffman and Ben Casnocha talk about how the best way to improve good qualities in yourself is to spend time with people who are already like that.

In choosing friends from a Christian writers' group, a Bible study, and creativity groups, I'd chosen wisely, becoming a better writer, growing stronger in my faith, and upping my creativity quotient by associating with other creatives. In other words, if you want to be more interesting, hang out with interesting people. If you want to be more creative, hang out with creative individuals. I experience a surge of creative energy in the room during each of my writing or creativity group meetings.

"When you find a people committed to a common mission, a common purpose, you find those individuals who are like-hearted and like-minded and carry the same fire you carry and whose passion burns as brightly as yours," Erwin Raphael McManus writes in *The Last Arrow*. "People don't slow you down; the *wrong* people slow you down. When you choose the right people, your life begins to come together in a way that it never could when you walk alone."

I also know what it is to feel pulled down by the wrong association. I've dropped out of groups that left me feeling depressed or anxious and learned to avoid people who pull me down into the muck and mire with them, spreading negative energy.

In her book *Living a Life You Love*, Joyce Meyer gives us permission to take a break from those who bring us down.

"In order to really give yourself a break," Joyce writes, "step away from people or things that bring you discouragement and sour your outlook on life . . . because they *will* affect you. There are just some people whom we need to love from a distance. If you have family members, friends, or coworkers whose constant negativity drains your joy and saps your peace, you probably need to create some distance. It doesn't mean you don't love them—it just means you need to give yourself a break."

McManus agrees. "The truth is, there *are* relationships that will keep you from the life God created you to live. There *are* people whom you need to extricate from your life because they pull you back to the person you were rather than forward to the person you must become," he writes. "Yet this must never blind us to the deeper truth. We were not created to do life alone, and if we want people to be for us, then there need to be people whom we are for."

Then there's the relationship that not only lifts but also builds a person: that of mentorship. I discovered what it was to have a mentor when I met author Shelly Beach.

"A mentor is someone who sees more talent and ability within you than you see in yourself, and helps bring it out of you," Bob Proctor, author, speaker, and success coach, describes it.

The first time I heard Shelly speak, I was entranced. I mentally took note of her mannerisms, the way she spoke from the heart, and how she referred to notes instead of reading from a prepared speech like some other presenters I'd seen.

I want to be like tha, I thought. *I want to be that kind of speaker.*

Through a desire to emulate her, I began reading Shelly's books and following her blog. I learned about the publishing world through her workshops. It was Shelly who advised me to drop the agent that represented my coupon book but had failed to submit to more than a handful of publishers. Shelly who would write a blurb endorsement for the book when it was finally released. And when I became a presenter at the same conference the following year, I discovered Shelly's speaking style came naturally to me.

I'm often asked about mentoring relationships in the writing classes I teach. "Ideally, the mentor would be someone further along in the writing field, someone knowledgeable who is also willing to share their wisdom and expertise," I tell them. My mind automatically goes to Shelly.

"How do I find a mentor?" someone will ask, and I'm tempted to answer "You don't. They find you," even though I'm aware that isn't completely accurate. The arrangement of mentorship can be a formal one through an organization or workplace, something loosely based that happens in a creative environment, or even cases when someone isn't aware they are serving as a mentor through their books, blogs, podcasts, or webinars.

Becoming Shelly Beach's protégé didn't feel like a strategic career move. Ours was not coincidental meeting. It was as though an invisible thread drew me to her, linking us irrevocably. A year later I would meet my second mentor, widely published author Cecil Murphey, under similar circumstances. I'm blessed that both Shelly and Cec have since become my close friends. I keep in touch with them through newsy letters, read their work, and feel free to seek their wise and experienced advice. I also count on them as my strongest prayer warriors. Knowing them has changed my life. Initially mentors, they are now "soul friends."

"Soul friends evoke, sustain, affirm, and unify us," Stephen Cope, psychotherapist and author of *Soul Friends: The Transforming Power of Deep Human Connection*, said. "A soul friend becomes critical to determining who we become as a person. They're people we form deep connections with. Connections that transform us. Soul friends call us forth. They draw out the person in us that we want to be. It's almost as if an invisible bond of energy connects us with these people."

I've experienced this same unexplained "connection" with others. One morning, while writing a letter to my friend Mary, I lamented that I'd never had a friend who could truly understand what it is to raise a large family. "I've never met a woman who believes, like I do, that children are a gift from God, a gift she couldn't say no to," I wrote. The next day I met a woman who introduced herself as a mother of nine. "Nine," I marveled. "That's one more than me."

"What other gift from God would we say no to?" she replied, and I'm certain my mouth dropped open as I recognized the very words I'd said that I'd never heard another woman say. Sheri became a cherished friend, and I became her writing mentor. I don't consciously choose these connections—it's as though they are chosen for me. I wonder sometimes if it is two souls recognizing each other, as they will in heaven.

Once I established relationships beyond my friend Mary, I needed to learn how to maintain them. Apparently, I couldn't just collect friends like pretty knickknacks, propping them on a shelf to be dusted off whenever I needed them.

According to Marquette University psychologist Debra Oswald, who has studied high school friendships, there are four basic behaviors necessary to maintain the bond of friendship. She discusses these in a November 2006 interview on PsychologyToday.com. The first two are self-disclosure and supportiveness. "We must be willing to extend ourselves, to share our lives with our friends, to keep them abreast of what's going on with us. Likewise, we need to listen to them and offer support." Consistent communication facilitates both these behaviors, whether it is through phone calls, emails, or the letter writing my friend Mary and I depended upon for over thirty years.

Another essential ingredient to keeping friends is being positive, according to Oswald. "The intimacy that makes a friendship thrive must be enjoyable, for the more rewarding a friendship, the more we're willing to expend the energy it takes to keep it alive."

The fourth essential ingredient to tending to a friendship is spending time together. What you do together doesn't seem to be as important as the regular interaction. Because some of my friendships are long-distance ones, I don't always have that luxury. In lieu of shared time, I've managed to maintain a connection in these long-distance friendships through postal mail. My interaction with Shelly and Cec has been relegated mostly to letter writing, while their return interaction is typically email.

I also practice gratitude through snail mail thank-you notes. I've written to former teachers, authors, and musicians whose work has touched my soul, or to businesses to laud praises upon their employees. I wrote the nurses who cared for David during cancer treatment, a mechanic who gave him a ride when his car broke down, and the staff at the funeral home that handled my mother's, husband's, and grandson's funerals with dignity and grace.

A short note can be handwritten and addressed in a few minutes, and the benefits reach both sender and receiver. A study at the University of Pennsylvania found that when participants were assigned to write and deliver a letter of gratitude, they immediately exhibited a huge increase in happiness scores, an effect that could last up to a month.

While there is no substitute for spending time with friends, our Ignite activity serves as a way to connect with a current friend, an avenue for reconnecting with an old one, or as a form of encouraging another person by taking advantage of snail mail.

Letters and notes can serve as a strong thread to keep friends connected. Never underestimate the power of a handwritten letter or note. My husband kept every single card that he received during his cancer treatment. I was poised to throw them away when, in November 2011, he unexpectedly asked to look through them. For one solid afternoon, he spent time poring over those notes and messages, celebrating his five-year cancer survival with the reminder of how much he meant to others.

Your assignment, should you accept it, is to **mail a card or letter to someone going through a tough time:** grieving the loss of a loved one, a job loss, a divorce, a cancer diagnosis. You shouldn't have to look too far around you to discover someone who could use something more than bills and advertisements in their mailbox to lift their spirits. Who knows? This simple act might spur you on to a card-sending campaign of saving the world one letter at a time. Here are **ten** other ways you can utilize the power of snail mail. Choose to do at least one, or challenge yourself to do all of them, in the next month:

1. **Write a thank-you note to someone who doesn't expect it but certainly deserves it.** Write to a former teacher, the nurse who did such a good job caring for your spouse, the barista at the coffee shop who never fails to smile. You might just make their day—maybe even their week.

2. **Write a letter or card to someone in the military.** The website "Operation We Are Here" (http://www.operationwearehere. com/IdeasforSoldiersCardsLetters.html) includes a listing of organizations that receive cards and letters to distribute to the military community, including deployed military personnel, wounded warriors, home front families, and veterans. Be sure to follow the instructions for specific organizations.

3. **Support a cancer patient.** Sign up to be a volunteer "Chemo Angel," becoming a buddy to a cancer patient currently undergoing treatment (https://www.chemoangels.com). You choose what type of angel you want to be: someone who sends notes and gifts throughout treatment, a card angel who commits to sending greeting cards, or a prayer angel. Another group is Girls Love Mail, sending letters and cards to women newly diagnosed with breast cancer (https://www.girlslovemail.com).

4. **Send cards to children in the hospital.** My grandson was five when he was diagnosed with cancer. Over the next three years, as he underwent treatment, he ended up in the hospital for days, weeks, and even more than a month after he underwent a stem cell transplant. Greeting cards, small toys, DVDs, and handheld game systems were invaluable to making the hospital bearable, for him and also for his mother, who slept on a couch in his room. Ask your local children's hospital how you can help cheer up a child's stay. In the patient's best interest, they have rules and regulations as to what they can accept, but even a cheery greeting card can go a long way in brightening a child's day. This group collects cards for hospitalized children: http://www.cardsforhospitalizedkids.com.

5. **Send gift cards to the parents of hospitalized children.** When you send greeting cards to children in the hospital, you might want to think about their parents too. While my grandson had meals served to him, my daughter had to eat food she brought, utilize the vending machines in the hospital, or go to a nearby café. The cost of gas to get back and forth to his many appointments and treatment was exorbitant too. Generous donations of gift cards for local coffee shops, fast food places, and gas stations were invaluable.

6. **Write to your children or grandchildren.** When I left home for college, I'd always check the mailbox at the dorm. My

parents and a couple sisters did not disappoint; that first year I received at least one letter a week. I still have those letters, some forty years later. Even when I lived a block away from my grandchildren, I'd surprise them with a card in the mailbox occasionally, or splurge and have a cookie bouquet delivered, always with a coupon code that made them affordable. Now that I live an hour away, it's even more important to keep in touch. I'm not one for FaceTiming, but I will make sure there's something in their mailbox from Grandma Mary.

7. **Mail a postcard to Postcrossing.** Like postcards? If you'd like to get postcards in your mailbox, you can register with Postcrossing (http://www.postcrossing.com). When you send a postcard, you'll receive a postcard back from another participant somewhere in the world. With nearly 800,000 members in 210 countries, approximately 350,000 postcards are traveling to mailboxes right now in this manner.

8. **Have a secret? Share it with PostSecret.** Whether it is a secret regret, fear, betrayal, desire, confession, or childhood humiliation, you can reveal anything, anonymously, on a postcard, briefly but creatively. This is a group art project, and shared postcard secrets can be viewed at www.postsecret.com, where you can also find the current address to send your secrets.

9. **Get creative with envelopes and stamps.** You can find envelope templates online, or take apart an envelope and lay it on an old map, decorated scrapbook paper, or even a page from your favorite magazine to cut out your own envelope pattern. Fold, and glue the edges shut. Use blank white address labels or a black marker to write the recipient's address. As for stamps, ask at the post office what designs are available and purchase those that add a little fun to your mailings.

10. **Find a snail mail pen pal.** Back when I was a young homeschooling mother of several children, magazines with pen pal

listings were plentiful. Not so much anymore, but there's still a large letter-writing community at "The Letter Exchange," https://letter-exchange.com/index.html, a forum that includes a print magazine, pen pal connection listings, and fun articles for fans of letter writing. A couple other forums for letter writers:

Letter Writer's Alliance: https://www.letterwriters.org
International Pen Friends: http://ipfworld.com

Creative Spark:
BILL POTTER

In the same trunk where I store my mother's letters, there is another stack rubber-banded together: those I received in the mid-seventies from the older brother I adored who was backpacking his way through the country. While I looked up to all my older siblings, Bill was the brother I perceived as the epitome of coolness during the bell-bottomed, long-haired '70s. The beautiful hand lettering on those letters attests to his artistic bent in high school, where he enjoyed sculpting in clay and designing black light posters.

Self-described as "rather rebellious and free-spirited" during that era, Bill left home after his 1973 high school graduation, two months before his eighteenth birthday, intent on reaching the Rocky Mountains with a friend who owned a car. When it looked as though their money was running out, the two then headed to Denver, Colorado, with their backpacks and tent, picking up odd jobs.

"Coming from small-town Iowa to the big city was an education on life," Bill says. "What I remember the most are the people I met there. I turned a bit 'hippie' as a result."

Bill soon returned to Iowa, where he worked at a factory for a couple of years before deciding to see more of the country. He hitchhiked his way to Portland, Oregon, where he picked fruit and did other odd jobs for two years, living without any more possessions than what he could carry on his back. Through his travels and occasional meals eaten at various churches and missions he visited in Denver and Portland, he was exposed to a different type of religion than the one he'd grown up with, hearing messages his troubled soul yearned for. He gave his heart to Jesus during one of the church's meetings. By the time he met his future wife, Brenda, in 1984, he'd returned to Iowa and was working as a truck driver. The two were baptized together.

"When we were first married, I was driving a truck over the road and normally home just on weekends," Bill says about that time. "Then when our daughter turned five, I took her with me for a week in the truck and realized just how awesome she was. It was then I decided I needed to find a different job that would allow me to be home with my new family."

Bill worked for a local hazardous chemical delivery company for a couple of years, then got another local delivery job, later moving into a mechanic position for that company. In 1994, by then a father of two, he began work as a mechanic with PMX Industries, the leading supplier of copper and copper alloys in North America. He was promoted to supervisor in 1998, then maintenance planner in 2000. He worked that position through the duration of his employment, retiring at age sixty-two.

"I owe my success at PMX to creativity. I've always liked creating or improving things, even as a mechanic," Bill says. "I know creativity helped me very much as a planner. I was responsible for designing machine downturn schedules, technical writing, and event planning. Although it wasn't part of my job description, I was still designing equipment improvements and sketching ideas for those improvements to become realities through the engineering and production departments."

While Bill had continued doing some drawing and writing through adulthood and enjoyed whittling during family campouts, it wasn't until he inherited our grandfather's tool chest that his creativity really took off.

"The chest was full of some of my mom's carving tools as well as a few of my grandpa's woodworking tools. Holding those tools in my hands, I thought about Mom and her father and the things they'd made. Using their tools made me feel like I was spending time with them. Once I started creating things (whittling, carving, and woodburning), it was like someone, maybe God himself, flipped on a switch, and now I can't stop creating," Bill says. "I feel so very blessed that I have an opportunity to do what I want to do and enjoy what I already have, not pursue 'more.' I get so much satisfaction from creating something. I can't see stopping as long as my fingers and mind function. I'm creating because I enjoy it, moved to do so by my Creator."

"Parenting is creating.
Teaching is creating.
Working is creating.
It all is."

—PATTI DIGH

O O	Jo Sheridan		
sold 1970	12 Virgin with baby Jesus, pine md. in 1969 darkened with Creosote, Des Moines	25	00
sold	13 Spanish St. Francis, oak Des Moines	45	00
sold	14 German Owl (Sleepy), walnut md. 1969 Des Moines	10	00
old	15 Spanish Bull #1, fir, stained black Des Moines	10	00
old	16 "Presentation" Madonna and baby, driftwood on walnut base, Des Moines	15	00
old	17 Owl in 2 colors of cedar, 8"h md. 1969 Des Moines	15	00
ld	18 Dancing bear, cedar, md. 1969 Pat + Marie Lenane, Dyersville, Ia.	8	00

When our mother was diagnosed with lung cancer in August 2010, my siblings and I had every reason to believe she'd live to see her eighty-third birthday the following February, with doctors predicting she could survive a year or more with treatment to slow the growth of lesions on her brain. Mom agreed to radiation only after the oncologist informed her the lesions would eventually affect speech and her ability to create.

"I have another painting in me," she told him.

Less than three months later, however, she was gone. If midlife means the midpoint of one's lifespan, my mother hit hers at forty-one, a year before she'd picked up a hammer and chisel to create her first wood carving. In the ensuing thirty years, Irma "Amy" Potter would produce 544 pieces of art, according to a ledger that tracked each piece. The entries are not dated, but they begin with the first wood carving in 1970 and end with the relief wood carving that was commissioned for the Delaware County courthouse in 1996. Anything Mom had crafted before the age of forty-two—the wall hangings, pastel pictures, quilts, or homemade dolls—were not included in this tally. Neither was the body of work she continued to produce between 1996 and her death in 2010. That includes countless pillows; teddy bears; baby quilts; Christmas stockings; handmade ornaments; a painting that hangs in Breitbach's restaurant in Balltown, Iowa; and lavishly designed walls my sister Pat commissioned Mom to paint in 2001 in the lower level of her Treasure Alley consignment store, along with numerous paintings and wood carvings now displayed in the homes of family members and strangers.

I could not begin to guess how many additional pieces of art my mother produced in those last fourteen years of her life, or why she stopped keeping the log, but suffice it to say, my mother was a prolific artist in the second half of her life.

Ironically, the valiant attempt to save her brain for that one last creation may have been the very thing that cut Mom's life short. Recuperating at home after completion of radiation treatment, she impatiently waited for her energy to return so she could begin the painting that existed only in her imagination. When my sister Joan stopped to check on her one late October day, she discovered Mom disoriented, confused, and too weak to go to the bathroom by herself. She went downhill fast, likely having suffered a stroke. Within days, our beautiful, brave mother was gone. Having lost our father some twenty-five years before, we were thrust into the role of orphans, feeling every bit the part. We lamented the loss collectively and individually, staggered by the enormity of our grief. One sister confessed to rocking back and forth on her couch, sobbing into a pillow Mom had made. Another who'd visited our mother several times a week seemed completely bereft without the regular visits.

From my youngest sister in her mid-forties to the oldest in her early sixties and the eight siblings in between, grief adversely affected our thinking patterns, muddling minds we believed were already experiencing glitches attributed to middle age: forgetting names, losing our keys, not being able to think of the right word. I remember talking to my sister Angie on the telephone one morning as I filled the washing machine in the basement. Later that same day, I stumbled around the house searching aimlessly for the ringing phone. I wondered what was wrong with my brain that I could lose a telephone I would later discover still in the basement.

Barbara Bradley Hagerty looks at the workings of the midlife brain in her book *Life Reimagined: The Science, Art, and Opportunity of Midlife*, quoting Mark McDaniel, a professor of psychology at Washington University in St. Louis.

"Almost every important neural aspect is declining with age," McDaniel said. "Neurochemically, physiologically, transmission interaction—all those things decline with age." Yet McDaniel and the other brain researchers Hagerty interviewed remained optimistic about middle age.

"I think midlife is the best time of all for your brain," neuroscientist Denise Park, director of the Center of Vital Longevity at the University of Texas, said. "You've reached a stage in your life where you have both cognitive resource—that is speed, memory, working memory, sort of mental horsepower—but at the same time you have knowledge, experience, and judgement. So I honestly believe in terms of your overall cognitive abilities, there's the wonderful blending of knowledge and cognitive resource that makes it probably the most efficient, effective time of your life."

That's encouraging for those of us worried that our brain has morphed into a duller version of its youthful counterpart. The good news is the adult brain seems to be capable of remodeling itself well into the prime of our life, incorporating decades of experience. Thanks to the Seattle Longitudinal study that tracked cognitive abilities of thousands of adults over fifty years, researchers have observed that midlife adults perform better on four out of six cognitive tests than those same individuals did as young adults. While memorization and perceptual skills do start to decline in young adulthood, verbal abilities, spatial reasoning, simple math activities, and abstract reasoning skills all improve in middle age.

According to Barbara Strauch, *New York Times* health editor and author of the book *The Secret Life of the Grown-Up Brain*, certain aspects of our thinking actually improve in midlife.

"Inductive reasoning and problem solving—the logical use of your brain and actually getting to solutions," Strauch writes. "We get the gist of an argument better. We're better at sizing up a situation and reaching a creative solution.

"What we have by middle age is all sorts of connections and pathways that have built up in our brain that help us," she said in a *New York Times* interview. "We used to think we lost thirty percent of our brain cells as we age. But that's not true. We keep them. That's probably the most encouraging finding about the physical nature of our brain cells."

Neuroscience has revealed that we are hardwired for lifelong learning, with research demonstrating that our brain remains plastic through its lifespan and can actually rewire itself when exposed to new and different activities.

Dr. Gene Cohen, responsible for the landmark 2001 "Creativity and Aging Study," discusses this in his book *The Creative Age.*

"We know that . . . the brain remains active—our 'wiring' remains flexible—and that it responds positively to challenge, creating new connections that strengthen our capacity to respond to new ideas and generate them," Cohen writes. "We know that creative stimulation enhances our health, both biologically and emotionally, and that some mental functions actually improve with age and experience. We know that even in the face of illness or disability, creative expression has the power to transform our lives with new opportunities and experiences of healing."

Mom's instinct to protect her precious brain was right on target then. As long as nothing happened to it, she could continue learning and creating. All her life she'd practiced creativity: in the way she'd stretched a small budget to feed and clothe her children, in the comfortable home she created, and through her art. Her artistic lifestyle likely buffered her against boredom and loneliness as she aged. A self-taught artist, my mother had continually challenged herself, by experimenting with different patterns in sewing projects and through wood carving, woodburning, watercolor, and acrylic and oil painting on barn boards and canvas. She'd craft quilts, dolls, teddy bears, tiny beaded strawberries, and miniature woolen mittens to hang on Christmas trees. She did copious amounts of research to fill notebooks with writing related to religion, faith, morality, history, and government. She kept folders of magazine and newspaper clippings and read books on topics that interested her. She never stopped learning. Had she not had the stroke, she likely would have continued to produce art and fill notebooks with writing until the day she died.

"Those people who have from the beginning developed complex lives with multiple interests and multiple talents, and continued to develop psychological complexity and tolerance for ambiguity, those people continue to do very well in later adulthood," Gary Gute, professor and director of the Creative Life Research Center at the University of Northern Iowa, said in a *Washington Post* article.

While it's never too late to begin a creative endeavor (Grandma Moses was in her late seventies when she began painting, after all), the neurological benefits to the brain seem to be most pronounced in people who began tapping into their artistic side in middle age, or before.

My siblings and I were in the thick of midlife when Mom died. Not only were we noticing a definite decline in our mental capacities after our mother's death, the demise of our last surviving parent also brought us face-to-face with our own mortality. Were my brothers and sisters conducting the same mental math equation I was? *Mom was eighty-two when she died on my fifty-first birthday. If I reach the same age, I have only thirty-one years left.*

Thoughts like that led me to question what I'd do with rest of my life. My mother's model of a lifetime of creativity and her admonition to utilize our God-given talents gave me the steely determination to take my writing seriously. I noticed my siblings taking similar paths: through quilting, genealogical research, painting, poetry, photography, and, for my brother Bill, the woodworking our mother and grandfather had modeled. The example of their grandmother's life and parents' artistic pursuits likely contributed to our children also pursuing creative endeavors. It seemed my mother's legacy of creativity had far-reaching implications in the lives of her children and grandchildren.

"To be creative in later life provides an invaluable model of what is possible as we age, for our children, grandchildren, great-grandchildren, and society," Dr. Cohen says. His study demonstrated how creative activities and skills mastery in a social environment had positive psychological, physical, and emotional benefits for older adults. "Most of us will never win the Nobel Peace Prize or a presidential election, but we can use creativity to shape our lives and, especially as we age, to unleash new potential for personal growth and self-expression."

That doesn't mean we have to completely reinvent ourselves or make a career out of artistic and creative endeavors to reap benefits. A four-year study headed by Dr. Rosebud Roberts at Mayo Clinic looked at people in their late eighties with normal cognitive levels. Those who engaged in artistic pursuits were 73 percent less likely to develop problems associated with mild cognitive impairments, including memory loss. Crafting activities, including ceramics, sewing, and woodworking, were associated with a 43 percent decrease in cognitive impairment risk, and engaging in socializing activities, such as book clubs, attending concerts, and traveling, was associated with a 55 percent decrease in developing cognitive impairments.

In my case, what began as a tribute to a creative mother would eventually become a complete transformation after my husband died. Anyone who knew me as a mostly stay-at-home mom just five years before—when my interactions with adults mainly consisted of choosing cuts of meat with the butcher at the grocery store and collecting stacks of letters from our mailman—wouldn't have imagined me as a workshop presenter or public speaker. A whole new world opened up to me after my husband's death, and I began doing things that David and I had only dreamed about experiencing after our children were raised. I traveled by airplane for the first time and attended my first concert. I signed six book contracts in the six years following David's death. I was chosen as keynote speaker for several events. I obtained certification as a grief counselor and founded an annual grief retreat. Yet I never felt qualified or personally responsible for any of these accomplishments. It all seemed to come from God.

"In a very real sense not one of us is qualified, but it seems that God continually chooses the most unqualified to do his work, to bear his glory," Madeleine L'Engle writes in *Walking on Water*. "If we are qualified, we tend to think that we have done the job ourselves. If we are forced to accept our evident lack of qualification, then there's no danger that we will confuse God's work with our own, or God's glory with our own."

"Are you happy?" one of my sons asked recently, surprising me with the seriousness of his question. My sons tend to joke about everything. Looking deep inside myself for the answer, I realized that despite missing his father and experiencing my share of daily stressors, I am. In the last few years, I've discovered a real sense of purpose in helping others navigate the dark path of grief. I love encouraging and educating beginning writers and conducting workshops. Doing presentations and speaking on topics I'm passionate about brings me immense joy. I never feel more alive than when I am doing presentations.

I'm not just happy, I've found *eudaimonia*. Loosely translated, the ancient Greek word means figuring out one's purpose in life, given their unique set of talents and capabilities, and pursuing goals that give their life meaning.

In the six months following the signing of the contract for this book, my life took some unexpected twists and turns, eerily paralleling the very topics I was writing about. My lifelong learners practiced the exercises that are included at the end of each chapter, serving as a beta test group to try new experiences, find time for play, and do things like strumming ukuleles or painting and making vision boards. Midway through working on the manuscript, in February 2018, I faced an unexpected and significant drop in income. It was quite a shock to discover that my reduced earnings wouldn't begin to cover all my bills. I had until the end of May to find a job with more hours or higher pay. I was devastated, until my daughter Elizabeth asked me what I would have done differently if I'd had forewarning of what was to come.

"Well, I wouldn't have quit the newspaper job that had more hours and health insurance," I replied. Even as I said it, I was struck by the realization that if I were still physically and creatively spent by the end of each day as a reporter, I would never have begun writing this book. I was suddenly grateful I hadn't known.

One of the positions I applied for in my quest for a different job was at a larger library. The first question I was asked by the pair of interviewers was "How did you prepare for this interview?"

Startled by the unexpected question, I blurted out the truth: "I prayed." The matching stunned looks on their faces left me certain I'd just ruined my chances for the job. Quickly recovering, I laughed nervously before adding, "I really didn't need to prepare; I know this job so well."

The rest of the interview went off without a hitch. When I was leaving the building, a young girl jumped out of a nearby parked car and ran across the street to hand me a Starbucks gift card. "Have a good day," she called out before running back to her vehicle. The random act of kindness felt like a warm hug, a message that everything would be okay. I got into my own vehicle, thinking again of the shocked looks on the faces of the two interviewers. I started giggling and was soon laughing out loud. I needed a job where I could comfortably be myself, and if my honest answer offended, then that wasn't the right one for me.

The next day I got a call from a spirituality center to set up an interview for the position of Program Coordinator. When I was offered the job, it felt as though I'd been preparing for it for years, as if everything I'd done since David's death had served as a stepping stone to this very job: planning programs for libraries, obtaining certification as a grief counselor, facilitating grief groups and a Bible study, and coordinating a grief retreat that had been hosted at their center. Even the newspaper job had provided me with writing experience, connections, and relationships I wouldn't have had otherwise. Not only would I be involved in one of my favorite activities—planning and conducting programs—I'd be free to talk daily about God and prayer, a dream come true for someone whose faith had become such a big part of her life.

"One of the interesting things we commonly see when people transform themselves later in life is that they're not just doing a new thing at a more or less mundane level," Dr. Michael Merzenich, a professor emeritus neuroscientist at the University of California, San Francisco, said in an interview with author Mark Walton, whose PBS program *Boundless Potential with Mark Walton* covers years of research on creativity. "We see that they have found what they're really meant to do in life and suddenly move into the domain they were really constructed for."

A few days after accepting the position, I studied the mind map I'd created weeks before, noting the words "new job" in the upper left-hand corner. I scrutinized the vision board that hung on my wall, with a leaf print, pictures of a sunset, a covered bridge, and mountains. It was obvious I'd desired more peace and nature in my life. I'd done both activities long before I got the job at a spirituality center that was situated adjacent to an eighty-one-acre prairie, with a meditation garden and ample space for walking, praying, and reflecting. I was acquiring my heart's desires with the change in employment.

Imagine the possibilities: a mostly stay-at-home, isolated mother of eight who could barely string two sentences together to communicate with the butcher and mailman now speaking in front of crowds, designing PowerPoints, and conducting workshops. After thirty years of writing articles and essays, that same woman somehow manages to sign six book contracts in the space of six years. If this woman's broken self, laid bare by grief, could learn to reach out to others and discover a job in midlife that fulfills *all* her passions, incorporating everything that her soul has been seeking, where might your search for meaning and purpose lead?

Isn't it time to find out?

"Follow your bliss and don't be afraid, and doors will open where you didn't know they were going to be."

—JOSEPH CAMPBELL

IGNITE

It's time to take action. Revisiting the Chapter 2 Ignite exercise, look at the list of creative endeavors you imagined yourself doing if time and money were no hindrance. Choose one to pursue this week or, if advance planning is required, this month. If you are conducting the exercises as a group, this might entail a field trip. Is there a creative endeavor several members of your group listed, like painting? Arrange for an art instructor to hold a painting class. Maybe this will be a solo effort and you'll try your hand at writing poetry. Purchase tickets for the train ride you've always wanted to take. Check out instructional YouTube videos or classes at a local community college. Your local library is full of possibilities with active learning and maker spaces and lifelong learning opportunities. Perhaps your action will be as an observer, and you'll head to an art museum or a concert to soak in the ambience and creative energy. It doesn't have to be something lofty or expensive. It could be as simple as choosing one of the books listed in the resource section of this book to read. Once you've chosen the first activity you will pursue, write it down as #1 on the following checklist. Add eleven more. You are committing to accomplishing just twelve things in your pursuit of a more creative life. Return to this list and check off those you accomplish, dating each one. Be in awe of what you can do once you set your mind to it.

Awesome Artistic Acts Checklist

☐ 1. _____

_____ Date _____

☐ 2. _____

_____ Date _____

☐ 3. _____

_____ Date _____

☐ 4. _____

_____ Date _____

☐ 5. _____

_____ Date _____

☐ 6. _____

_____ Date _____

☐ 7. _____

_____ Date _____

☐ 8. _____

_____ Date _____

☐ 9. _____

_____ Date _____

☐ 10. _____

_____ Date _____

☐ 11. _____

_____ Date _____

☐ 12. _____

_____ Date _____

"To live is the rarest
thing in the world.
Most people exist,
that is all."

—OSCAR WILDE

Creative Spark:
ALLISON POSTER

In August 2017, I spoke on "The Legacy of Creativity" at the Inspire Café in Dubuque, talking about my mother, her art, and the creativity that resides within each one of us. It wasn't my first visit to the café, but I'd never seen the beautiful art that was displayed on the walls before. I asked about the pieces when I purchased my drink and was informed that they'd begun showcasing local artists; everything there belonged to an artist named Allison Poster.

I moved closer to study the mixed media pieces, something deep within me resonating with the images of butterflies, angels, trees, and hummingbirds on old mirrors and windows and a framed image of a hauntingly sad girl in a birdcage. I was fascinated by the artist's use of broken and crushed glass, bits and pieces of old jewelry, and repurposed frames. I snapped a photo of the piece titled "Hummingbird Reflections" to share with my daughter Elizabeth. I knew there had to be a story behind the art.

I picked up Allison's business card and searched for her Facebook page so I could message her to tell her how beautiful her art was and let her know I hoped to hear her story someday. Two years later, thanks to another creative woman, I did.

Each time I drove by the future home of Upcycle Dubuque, I'd wonder about the business name, thinking it might be something related to art. I connected with co-owner Kristina Beytien as soon as I discovered that the mission of the store was one of upcycling and recycling, a concept I hoped to share in the creativity group at my workplace. A creative reuse scrap store in back, the front portion of the store would include an art gallery featuring local artisans. When it finally opened for business, Kristina's artfully done storefront window immediately captured my attention. The first time I set foot in the store, Allison Poster's hummingbird welcomed me from the wall, where it was displayed with several of her other pieces. I knew then: It was time to meet this artist.

"We all have creativity within. It's about connecting with ourselves through art," Allison opens our conversation. "I want to take things that are broken and create beauty."

That includes her broken self.

Allison was six years old when she started picking her skin. Known as excoriation disorder or *dermatillomania*, chronic skin picking is a body-focused repetitive behavior related to obsessive-compulsive disorder.

"I grew up one of eight children on a farm," Allison says, choosing her next words carefully. "I lived in a very chaotic household. Feelings were not okay. I started picking at my skin to numb out feelings."

Age six was when Allison's sexual abuse by a relative began. At thirteen, she had her first panic attack. She struggled with anxiety and depression well into adulthood, seeking therapy in her thirties. By then, she was married and working as a nurse. Pursuing creativity facilitated her healing process as her therapist assigned artwork to help her through what she was unable to express verbally.

Allison had always loved art, even into high school, imagining she could become an artist someday. Then in ninth grade, she was encouraged to choose a profession. "I got the idea that art wasn't one, so I chose nursing," Allison says. "Then when my daughter was born fourteen years ago, I couldn't afford the Pottery Barn decorating, so I looked at what I liked and began painting."

Using acrylics on canvas, she painted a ladybug on a stem and a flower that would match her daughter's pink room. Later, she did a train, plane, and car for her son Isaac's room, and for her twins, two monkeys hanging upside down with a lion and a giraffe. Her friends began asking for paintings for their children's rooms. Her husband gifted her with a drawing and painting class. She branched out to mixed media, learning from Pinterest and YouTube videos. When a friend asked her to paint on two old windows, she had to do research to figure out how to paint on glass, but once she learned, she never looked back, loving the idea of repurposing materials that might otherwise end up in a landfill.

Before long, she was displaying pieces at gallery shows. She rented an art studio at Dubuque Studio Works and was a featured artist for them.

While Allison still works one day a week as a nurse at Unity Point Clinics, the rest of her time is spent on creating art or teaching one-on-one classes with students. She's also begun telling her story so her experience can help others.

"I'm a huge advocate of mental health," she says. "Creativity is grounding. I release my emotions through my painting. There is lightness and darkness in every piece. My spirituality is so much stronger since I began looking at the darkness."

"Years ago, I couldn't even imagine I could have an art studio or speak in front of crowds," Allison adds. "It blows my mind. That has to come from God. My spiritual self is within each of the pieces I do."

Allison's art can be found on Facebook under AllisonPostersPersonalizedFineTreasures.

— ◆ —

Of all the art forms practiced by my creative sparks, none spoke to me in the way that Allison Poster's mixed media pieces did. I was already familiar with painting from high school, ukulele playing was not my forte, the practice of yoga didn't particularly appeal to me, and I had no desire to work with wood like my brother.

Perhaps it was the former dumpster-diving coupon queen in me that was attracted to the tiny bits and pieces of "trash" incorporated into Allison's art. Maybe it was regret at losing so many pieces of my life through the deaths of mother, husband, and grandson in the space of three years or the radical move to a much smaller home. Whatever it was, something from deep within me was drawn to her work. By the time I finally met the artist, I'd already begun collecting small things that could be included in a piece of my own: Mom's holy medals and her broken rosary with a blue cross, representative of her deep Catholic faith. A vintage book of poetry about mothers, with yellowed pages of quaint illustrations and poetry of days gone by. I had newspaper clippings about her artwork. A pillowcase with her careful embroidered stitching. The last chalk pastel drawing that remained on her easel after her death. Then there was the yellow rose I'd painted at age sixteen, the same age as my youngest daughter now. I'd sat next to my mother in her workroom as I'd painted it. Pleased with the rose but never with the background, I'd given it to Mom for her birthday and she'd framed it. (For more than forty years I'd been embarrassed by that background. Was there a way to utilize the rose and cover part of it? Artist Allison assured me there was.) Finally, there was the "magic pencil" I'd found in my mother's empty house. I'd ordered hundreds of similar pencils on eBay to give away when I did presentations on creativity but remained fearful of losing the original. What if the pencil could be immortalized in some way? Allison beamed with pleasure at my inspired suggestion.

I had all these pieces and an artist willing to guide me, yet I remained fearful, the very idea of trying my hand at creating a mixed media piece terrifying me, something so new and different than anything I'd attempted before. What if I ruined the pieces I'd chosen to include with adhesive? What if the final product looked terrible, or nothing like I imagined when I even dared to imagine a mixed media piece created in honor of my mother?

The fear was real. It dawned on me then just what I was asking readers of this book to do—open up their minds to creative possibilities, try new things, and allow for the possibility of failure, all in the name of discovering their true nature, their God-given potential, the creative self within them. How dare I suggest something I was not willing to do myself? I suddenly knew I *must* create this one piece, regardless of how it turned out or whether I ever attempted mixed media again. I needed to step outside of my comfort zone and do exactly what I was asking my readers to do. This is the result.

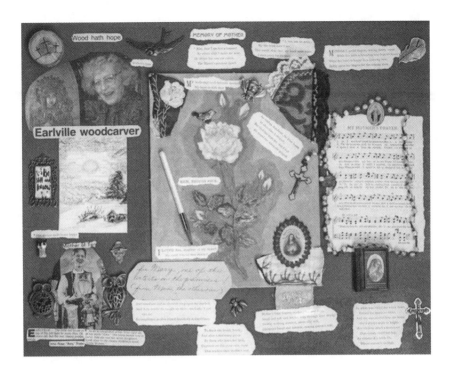

Shortly after I completed this piece, I met with a new friend who'd lost his wife the year before. Listening closely to the answers he gave to my questions, I realized how many times he used the word "can't" or "I'd never" in our conversation. I immediately sensed there was more to my creation than I'd realized.

"Did you see that mixed media piece I created to represent my book's message that I posted on Facebook?" I asked. He had. "That's what our life is like: little bits and broken pieces. Everything we went through and experienced up until that moment when our beloved took their last breath. There are ugly moments we'd rather not remember and beautiful ones. There are precious memories. There is a pattern to our life that has made us who we are. Picture your life as a mixed media collage. Whatever you add to the collage from this point forward is up to you. You can keep moving those broken parts around. You can add similar pieces. That is your comfort zone, and there is nothing wrong with that. There's a reason it's called the comfort zone; it's comfortable. Safe.

"But God might have something more for you, and if you continue saying 'I can't' or 'I'd never,' you are essentially saying 'NO.' God's plans for you are so much bigger than what you can ever imagine for yourself. He can use you in so many ways if you let him. You can grow in him and share in the masterpiece he wants to make of your life's collage."

Is God asking you to do something today? Is there something you are feeling led to that sounds too difficult, is uncomfortable, or you don't feel qualified for?

What might you be saying "NO" to?

"Ordinary women become extraordinary when they find a way to tap into the wellspring of creativity."

—EILEEN M. CLEGG

Chapter 12:
THE GREAT COLLABORATOR

◆

Success ... will only be known after I die -if I have helped anyone
get to Heaven and. if I get to Heaven. Our main purpose on earth is to
save our soul and try to do the Will of God in all things. That also
means using the talents that God gives us and using them for good.

◆

After our mother's house sold, I'd worried that the loss of my private writing retreat and her table would mean an end to the surge of creative energy I'd experienced in those three months. Instead, the intensity of those weeks of writing sessions only served to invigorate me, practicing creativity begetting even more creativity. As I discovered, meeting with other creatives can do the same thing.

"Finding like-minded creative friends is important for those seminal imaginative sparks to catch fire," Grant Faulkner writes in *Pep Talks for Writers*. "'None of us is as smart as all of us,' the saying goes. An initial idea grows through the interchange of ideas, with one idea sparking another idea—and then the light bulb of inspiration glows."

Investing time and money into a writing conference in the summer of 2011 was a big step for me. With an agent pitching my completed manuscript, it may have been the first time I considered myself a "real" writer, despite the fact that I'd been selling articles and essays for more than twenty years. With the investment, I was primed to learn more about the business side of publishing and what it is to join a community of writers who are willing to share ideas and experiences, encouraging each other. Garnering like-minded friends and a mentor in Shelly Beach was just an added bonus. David reveled in the writing I was doing and the relationships I'd formed. You would have thought all of it was of his making.

A series of awe-inspiring events that followed my husband's death led me to my second mentor, Cecil Murphey, an author whose book *90 Minutes in Heaven* David had read and recommended to me.

It was unusual for David to be the one to recommend a book. I'd always been the reader in our marriage, and until that last year of his life, he counted on me to choose his reading material: books by Philip Gulley, Bill Bryson, and Dave Barry and biographies of famous people. It was completely out of character, then, when in the months preceding his death, David began reading books by televangelist Joyce Meyer. I knew he'd been watching her on television, so I shouldn't have been surprised. Most mornings I came downstairs to find him already on the couch, watching one of her broadcasts.

Though he'd ask me to join him, I usually headed straight to the kitchen to get some writing in before the kids woke up. What did he find so appealing about her message that he'd also wanted to read her books? I remember watching with him only once, when curiosity had gotten the best of me.

It was just weeks before he died. We sat on the couch next to each other, holding hands. I immediately saw the appeal in Joyce's down-to-earth attitude. I found her to be a dynamic speaker, so I was taken aback when David suddenly turned to me, proclaiming I would someday "be like her." Though I'd done a few workshops by then, I never imagined becoming a public speaker. Then he scrutinized my hair. "And I want you to go to the hairdresser as often as you need, to look good for your public."

I was flabbergasted. My husband was imagining something I couldn't fathom: believing not only that I would someday be a speaker but that I'd *have a public*. As for the hair comment, apparently before I'd joined him on the couch, Joyce had discussed her frequent visits to the hairdresser. To this day, I can rationalize hairstylist visits before a big event, knowing my husband would have approved.

When David had a heart attack in mid-March, I brought several books and magazines to the hospital for him to read, but he'd waved them away, saying he didn't have the energy. The day before he was to be released, he asked about the book I'd brought for myself.

"Leave that for me," he said when I told him the title. I was surprised, since he'd made it clear up to then that he hadn't wanted any reading material. When I packed his things for home the next morning, the book was on top of a nearby shelf. I never asked, and he didn't mention it, so I'll never know if he actually read any of it, but I do know *Getting to Heaven* by Cecil Murphey and Don Piper was the last book David touched.

Three days after his return from the hospital, my husband died during the night. When the mail was delivered to my house that morning, someone retrieved it from the mailbox, dropping it in my lap. Numbly, I thumbed through it. Beside greeting cards from David's siblings for what would have been his birthday the following day, there was an envelope from Cecil Murphey's assistant, Twila Belk. Inside was a check for $50 along with notification that an essay I wrote would be appearing in an anthology compiled by Murphey and Belk. Two days later, on the evening of my husband's wake, I received an email awarding me a Cecil Murphey scholarship for the upcoming Write-to-Publish writing conference in Wheaton, Illinois. When I'd filled out the application, I'd asked David what we would do if I won, since the conference ended on our June anniversary.

"There will be other anniversaries," he'd commented, insisting I apply.

My first contact with the man whose name kept appearing in my life would be an exchange of emails in which I explained my recent loss and his return reassurance that I could use the scholarship another year, if needed. I finally decided it would be easiest to spend my first lone wedding anniversary away from my home, doing something David had wanted for me. I never imagined the conference would be more a spiritual than educational experience.

While I'd prayed and asked God to pair me up with another widow in the dorm room, he knew better what I needed. My roommate was a woman who'd never married or had children. While friendly enough, she left me completely to my own devices, which allowed me quiet and solitude. She seemed completely oblivious to the tear-stained cheeks I woke up with (inexplicably escaping from my eyes as I slept) or my muffled sobs into a washcloth in the shower on the morning of what would have been my anniversary. Nor was she in the room anytime I wanted breathing space between sessions. Much of the conference was a blur in grief-induced fog, but certain moments remain crystal clear.

I remember the beautiful music that began each morning and had me bolting from the room in tears. I'll never forget author Jane Rubietta who found me in the hallway and took hold of my hands to pray for me, or Cynthia Ruchti's workshop that I ended up in by accident, with a message I copied down so I can share it now. "Life . . . even with its distressing parts . . . feeds our words and ignites our stories. God doesn't waste anything. Let the Lord use it. God will refresh you and revive you," she said as a lump formed in my throat and tears filled my eyes. "Brave writers all write from a dwelling place, or a history of pain. Mine the pain. Don't waste it. Use it."

I don't have to search my memory for the sign I discovered the final day of the conference because I've saved it as a reminder. The piece of paper—that hadn't been there just moments before—was attached to a tree on a pathway that reminded me of the University of Northern Iowa campus I'd walked with David the previous year. The handwritten sign declared: *If a tree does not suffer great winds and storms, its bark will not grow thick and strong. The tree, thin, naked, and weak, will fall over and die. Storms will bring strength, majesty, and growth. God brings storms to build us. When He builds us, we will go forward.* I carefully removed it from the bark, certain its message was meant for my wounded soul, just as that morning's guest pastor's devotional had been.

"I see you, Mary." His booming voice startled me at the back of the room, and his eyes seemed to look straight into mine, yet I'd never met him and was convinced he'd chosen a random common name. "I see you, Mary. Take courage. Be filled with courage. Every follower of Jesus Christ can survive their deep water and dark night experiences because we have the knot of reassurance that even when we can't see Jesus, Jesus sees us. 'I am here. I am here for you,' he says. Don't be afraid to take the next step."

Thanks to the conference, I knew my next step: I'd be writing a book about grief.

That fall, I traveled to the Maranatha Christian Writers' Conference to personally meet and thank the man who was responsible for the scholarship I'd won. I arrived at the conference just before the evening meal was to be served. The coordinator left me in the empty cafeteria, assuring me other attendees would soon be there. I filled a cup of coffee and set it at an empty table in front of a chair where I placed my purse. My back to the tables, I slowly began filling a plate from the buffet. When I turned around, I saw that a man with a full head of white hair had taken the seat next to the one

I'd claimed. I'd seen photos of Cecil Murphey. Surely it couldn't be possible that with all those empty tables and chairs in the room, he'd somehow chosen the one next to mine?

He glanced up as I approached, and I gasped.

"Cecil Murphey? I can't believe it! You're the person I've come here to see!" When I clasped his outstretched hand, I swore I felt an immediate jolt of recognition, as if our souls already knew each other. In the next few days, I took several of his workshops, learning from a writing pro and observing a speaking style that was uncannily similar to that of our mutual friend Shelly Beach. Shelly had arranged for Cec and I to share an evening meal, an overnight stay at the same bed and breakfast, and a ride to the airport the next morning. By the time I hugged him goodbye, I'd gained another mentor and friend.

Six months later, Cec's wife died. A year ahead of him in grief, I yearned to help my new friend down a path I'd already traveled. While I'd been writing to him occasionally, I amped up the frequency of my letters. I sent him books I'd found helpful and pieces of my work in progress, the book I'd begun at the conference his scholarship had gifted me with. Our friendship was strengthened by this bond of mutual loss, and Cec would eventually write the foreword for that book. The year after it was released, my new mentor was the keynote speaker for the Cedar Falls conference. While in Iowa, he officiated at the backyard wedding of my son Dan and his fiancée, Lydia.

When I discovered Cec would be returning to Iowa in April 2016 and was searching for speaking engagements while here, I was stunned to realize the timing of his visit would coincide with a grief speech I'd been contracted for a year in advance. The coordinator readily accepted the addition of the famous author as a co-speaker.

The opportunity to speak with my mentor was a dream come true. I had no doubt that an outline and our similar speaking styles would guide us in meshing our grief stories. A practice session at a small church gathering the night before went well. We said a prayer together before we stepped on stage the next evening for the big event.

Something extraordinary happened during the final portion of the speech with my mentor. At one point I distinctly remember wondering where my words were coming from. I saw several people in the audience wiping away tears as I spoke. When Cec gently tugged at my sleeve to indicate we needed to culminate the presentation, I protested lightly. When he leaned over and whispered that I'd been talking for twenty minutes, I was astonished, realizing there was no time for our planned wrap-up. Cec deftly closed with some final remarks. A group of women approached me as he headed to the hallway where a display of our books was set up.

"I wish he hadn't stopped you," one woman said, and the others nodded. "You were saying exactly what I needed to hear."

I almost asked her what I'd said, as I had no recollection. Instead, I listened to their concerns and answered their questions for another half hour. By the time I made it to the sales table, the crowd had dissipated. When Cec apologized for cutting me short, I confidently assured him that whoever needed to hear more had stayed behind. I didn't explain what had happened, because I wasn't sure myself. While I'd experienced something similar with my writing on occasion—when something outside of myself takes over—this was the first time I'd experienced it with a speech. It wouldn't be the last. When it does happen, I thank God for the phenomenal occurrence. While it sounds lofty (*Oh, that wasn't me talking—that was God*), it is the opposite. It is acknowledging that I couldn't possibly be responsible for my successes on my own. Instead, I've allowed the Holy Spirit to lead. I've since discovered others have experienced the same thing.

"Have you ever had a moment when you knew you were awesome? I know you are not supposed to say that, but have you ever thought it? You know, that moment when everything just came together. You were in perfect form," Erwin McManus writes in *The Artisan Soul*. "Athletes call it 'the zone'; in other disciplines they call it 'finding your flow.' As a speaker, it's the moment when you don't even have to think. The words seemingly form themselves."

Thomas Kinkade experienced it while painting. "The more deeply involved I become in the act of creation, however, the more

I have the sense that the most creative work I do is not really my own—that the ideas and the expression come from outside or beyond me. At times I've had the sense that I was holding the brush but that a power outside myself was guiding my hand," he wrote in *Lightposts for Living.*

"You may know this feeling. It's the feeling you get when you've made something wonderful, or done something wonderful, and when you look back at it later, all you can say is: 'I don't even know where that came from,'" Elizabeth Gilbert writes in *The Big Magic.* "Sometimes, when I'm in the midst of writing, I feel like I am suddenly walking on one of those moving sidewalks that you find in a big airport terminal; I still have a long slog to my gate, and my baggage is still heavy, but I can feel myself being gently propelled by some exterior force. Something is carrying me along—something powerful and generous—and that something is decidedly not *me.*"

This is what can happen when our work becomes a form of worship with the Creator as our collaborator. In *Walking on Water,* Madeleine L'Engle described her process of writing this way: "To work on a book is for me very much the same thing as to pray. Both involve discipline. If the artist works only when he feels like it, he's not apt to build up much of a body of work. Inspiration far more often comes during the work than before it, because the largest part of the job of the artist is to listen to the work and go where it tells him to go."

Most of us will probably not make a living from our creative endeavors. There's a reason I keep a day job, which offers its own opportunities for creativity and innovation. Some readers will have been fortunate to discover a purpose in life during their youth. Others will have struggled for years to become what they are meant to become, holding down dead-end jobs or fighting frustration as they valiantly attempt to stoke that tiny flame that burns within. Then there are those facing the tail end of life, restless with the certainty that there is something yet to be accomplished. The remaining, like my mother and great-aunt Christine, already incorporate creativity and faith in every part of their lives.

"Every day God invites us on the same kind of adventure. It's not a trip where He sends us a rigid itinerary, He simply invites us. God asks what it is He's made us to love, what it is that captures our attention, what feeds that deep indescribable need of our souls to experience the richness of the world He made. And then, leaning over us, He whispers, 'Let's go do *that* together,'" Bob Goff, founder of Love Does, once wrote.

In the end, my mother's life had been her finest masterpiece, her legacy.

What will yours be?

Dec. 2005
The most important moment of life is the End of it.

VIGNETTE

It was an unseasonably warm October day. Mom and I had conversed comfortably in the car on the way to and from her radiation appointment—about my recent blog posts that mentioned her, the LIVE *sign I'd purchased, and her concern over her cat being attacked by some feral felines. I'd assumed if she wanted to discuss more serious topics, she'd have brought them up. Back at her house, I helped her out of the car. She swayed a little as she stood, and I grabbed her arm to steady her. She clung to me as we made our way to the back door. Mom expressed the desire to stay outside, so I settled her in a chair before getting her coffee and cigarettes. Setting them on the small white table in front of her, I asked if she'd be alright if I headed home to make supper for David and the children. She assured me she would. I can remember leaning down to kiss her cheek, and while I'm certain I would have told her I loved her, I can't recall actually saying the words.*

Once inside the car, I started the engine before glancing back at Mom. She was looking straight at me, a smile on her face. She raised her hand slightly, giving a little wave. It was that one small gesture that undid me. My throat filled with tears and I could barely breathe. I looked away so she wouldn't see me cry. My mother is dying, *I thought as I headed down the driveway.* My mother is dying. *I sobbed all the way home.*

There is so much we didn't talk about that day. In fact, we hadn't mentioned death or dying in any of our conversations since her diagnosis. I'd been with her when the doctor informed her she had lung cancer, had heard her whisper "I wondered what it would be." We never talked about fear, or even faith, which surprised me, considering how important religion was to her.

More than six years after her death, in early 2017, when I reread letters Mom had written, her Memory Book, and the odd notebooks and partial journals I'd inherited, I realized she'd already said it all, had managed to impart her faith and knowledge in the life she'd lived. There was nothing more to say. Her last lesson was in facing death with dignity, grace, and the firm belief she would soon be joining both our father and Our Father.

She surprised me, this mother of mine, appearing in this manuscript in ways I had not imagined, her words neatly written in her perfect penmanship. It was a delight when my father unexpectedly made an appearance in the ninth chapter, and it was healing when a poem about my grandson erupted from the ashes of grief.

As I culminate months of writing, in my mind's eye, I see my mother sitting outside at that little table, a cigarette in her hand, a cup of coffee in front of her. Her face is lit by a beatific smile, her eyes filled with love. She lifts her hand, giving a little wave.

"I love you, Mom," I say this time, waving back.

I gave my life, but until it was finished, no one can know what that life gave.

My death is not mine. It is yours. It will mean what you make of it. Whether my life and death was for good or for nothing, it is you who must say this.

I leave you my death. Give it meaning. Remember me."

IGNITE

Now that you've completed this book, decide how you will incorporate creativity in your life to become happier and healthier and live your life to the fullest. Circle the steps that you have already taken, underline those you'd like to try, and then add your own in the space provided.

- I will remind myself of those things I loved doing as a child.

- I will think outside the box.

- I will schedule time to create.

- I will give myself regular periods of solitude.

- I will try new things.

- I will allow myself to fail.

- I will surround myself with things that bring me joy.

- I will be mindful of my moments.

- I will be kinder.

- I will help others.

- I will practice gratitude.

- I will find my tribe, a group that feeds my soul.

- I will leave a legacy of creativity.

Add your own:

-

-

-

-

-

-

-

-

-

-

-

-

-

-

-

RESOURCES

Books

Beck, Martha. *Finding Your Way in a Wild New World: Reclaim Your True Nature to Create the Life You Want*. New York: Free Press, 2012.

Brits, Louisa Thomsen. *The Book of Hygge: The Danish Art of Contentment, Comfort, and Connection*. New York: Plume, 2017.

Cameron, Julia. *The Artist's Way: A Spiritual Path to Higher Creativity*. New York: TarcherPerigee, 2016.

Carson, Shelley. *Your Creative Brain: Seven Steps to Maximize Imagination, Productivity, and Innovation in Your Life*. San Francisco, CA: Jossey-Bass, 2012.

Clegg, Eileen M. *Claiming Your Creative Self: True Stories from the Everyday Lives of Women*. Oakland, CA: New Harbinger Pub. Inc, 1999.

Cohen, Gene D. *The Creative Age: Awakening Human Potential in the Second Half of Life*. New York: William Morrow, 2001.

Cope, Stephen. *Soul Friends: The Transforming Power of Deep Human Connection*. Carlsbad, CA: Hay House Inc., 2017.

Csikszentmihalyi, Mihaly. *Flow: The Psychology of Optimal Experience*. New York: Harper & Row, 1990.

DeMuth, Mary E. *Thin Places: A Memoir*. Grand Rapids, MI: Zondervan, 2010.

Emmons, Robert. *Thanks! How the New Science of Gratitude Can Make You Happier*. New York: Houghton Mifflin, 2007.

Faulkner, Grant. *Pep Talks for Writers: 52 Insights and Actions to Boost Your Creative Mojo*. San Francisco, CA: Chronicle Books, 2017.

Frankl, Sara, and Mary Carver. *Choose Joy: Finding Hope and Purpose When Life Hurts*. New York: FaithWords, 2016.

Friedman, Howard S., and Leslie R. Martin. *The Longevity Project: Surprising Discoveries for Health and Long Life from the Landmark Eight-Decade Study*. New York: Hudson Street Press, 2011.

Gilbert, Elizabeth. *Big Magic: Creative Living Beyond Fear*. New York: Riverhead Books, 2015.

Gladwell, Malcom. *Outliers: The Story of Success*. New York: Little, Brown and Company, 2008.

Goff, Bob. *Love Does: Discover a Secretly Incredible Life in an Ordinary World.* Nashville, TN: Thomas Nelson, 2012.

Greenhalgh, Wendy Ann. *Stop Look Breathe Create.* London: Octopus Publishing Group, 2017.

Hagerty, Barbara Bradley. *Life Reimagined: The Science, Art, and Opportunity of Midlife.* New York: Riverhead Books, 2016.

Hatmaker, Jen. *Of Mess and Moxie: Wrangling Delight Out of This Wild and Glorious Life.* Nashville, TN: Nelson Books, 2017.

Hoffman, Reid, and Ben Casnocha. *The Start-up of You: Adapt to the Future, Invest in Yourself, and Transform Your Career.* New York: Currency, 2012.

Kaufman, Scott Barry, and Carolyn Gregoire. *Wired to Create: Unraveling the Mysteries of the Creative Mind.* New York: TarcherPerigee, 2016.

Kenyon, Mary Potter. *Expressive Writing for Healing: Journal Your Way from Grief to Hope.* Sanger, CA: Familius, 2018.

Kinkade, Thomas. *The Art of Creative Living: Making Every Day a Radiant Masterpiece.* New York: Warner Faith, 2005.

Kinkade, Thomas. *Lightposts for Living: The Art of Choosing a Joyful Life.* New York: Warner Books, 1999.

Kleon, Austin. *Steal Like an Artist: 10 Things Nobody Told You About Being Creative.* New York: Workman, 2012.

Kondo, Marie. *The Life-Changing Magic of Tidying Up: The Japanese Art of Decluttering and Organizing.* Berkeley, CA: Ten Speed Press, 2014.

Kondo, Marie. *Spark Joy: An Illustrated Master Class on the Art of Organizing and Tidying Up.* Berkeley, CA: Ten Speed Press, 2016.

Land, George, and Beth Jarman. *Breakpoint and Beyond: Mastering the Future Today.* New York: HarperBusiness, 1992.

Langer, Ellen J. *On Becoming an Artist: Reinventing Yourself through Mindful Creativity.* New York: Ballantine Books, 2006.

L'Engle, Madeleine, and Luci Shaw. *Friends for the Journey.* Ann Arbor, MI: Vine Books, 1997.

L'Engle, Madeleine. *Walking on Water: Reflections on Faith and Art.* New York: Convergent Books, 2016.

Levy, Mark. *Accidental Genius: Using Writing to Generate Your Best Ideas, Insight, and Content,* 2nd Edition. San Francisco, CA: Berrett-Koehler Publishers, 2010.

Lyubomirsky, Sonja. *The How of Happiness: A Scientific Approach to Getting the Life You Want*. New York: The Penguin Press, 2007.

MacLeod, Hugh. *Ignore Everybody: And 39 Other Keys to Creativity*. New York: Portfolio, 2009.

Magnusson, Margareta. *The Gentle Art of Swedish Death Cleaning: How to Free Yourself and Your Family from a Lifetime of Clutter*. New York: Scribner, 2018.

Maisel, Eric. *A Writer's Space: Make Room to Dream, to Work, to Write*. Avon, MA: Adams Media, 2008.

McManus, Erwin Raphael. *The Artisan Soul: Crafting Your Life into a Work of Art*. New York: HarperOne, 2014.

McManus, Erwin Raphael. *The Last Arrow: Save Nothing for the Next Life*. New York: WaterBrook, 2017.

Meyer, Joyce. *Living a Life You Love: Embracing the Adventure of Being Led by the Holy Spirit*. New York: FaithWords, 2018.

Michaels, Melissa. *Love the Home You Have: Simple Ways to Embrace Your Style, Get Organized, Delight in Where You Are*. Eugene, OR: Harvest House Publishers, 2015.

Oliver, Mary. *Upstream: Selected Essays*. New York: Penguin Press, 2016.

Penman, Danny. *The Art of Breathing: The Secret to Living Mindfully*. Newburyport, MA: Conari Press, 2018.

Penman, Danny. *Mindfulness for Creativity: Adapt, Create and Thrive in a Frantic World*. London: Piatkus Books, 2015.

Pennebaker, James E. & Smyth, Joshua M. *Opening Up by Writing it Down: How Expressive Writing Improves Health and Eases Emotional Pain*. New York: The Guilford Press, 2016.

Proctor, Bob. *The ABCs of Success: The Essential Principles from America's Greatest Prosperity Teacher*. New York: Tarcher/Putnam, 2015.

Progoff, Ira. *At a Journal Workshop: Writing to Access the Power of the Unconscious and Evoke Creative Ability*. New York: Tarcher/Putnam, 1992.

Rubin, Gretchen. *Happier at Home: Kiss More, Jump More, Abandon a Project, Read Samuel Johnson, and My Other Experiments in the Practice of Everyday Life*. New York: Three Rivers Press, 2012.

Rubin, Gretchen. *The Happiness Project: Or, Why I Spent a Year Trying to Sing in the Morning, Clean My Closets, Fight Right, Read Aristotle, and Generally Have More Fun*. New York: Harper Collins, 2009.

Schaefer, Edith. *The Hidden Art of Homemaking: Creative Ideas for Enriching Everyday Life*. Wheaton, IL: Tyndale House, 1985.

Schweiger, Rebecca. *Release Your Creativity: Discover Your Inner Artist with 15 Simple Painting Projects*. New York: Get Creative 6, 2017.

Stoddard, Alexandra. *Choosing Happiness: Keys to a Joyful Life*. New York: William Morrow, 2002.

Stoddard, Alexandra. *Living a Beautiful Life: 500 Ways to Add Elegance, Order, Beauty and Joy to Every Day of Your Life*. New York: Random House, 1986.

Strauch, Barbara. *The Secret Life of the Grown-Up Brain: The Surprising Talents of the Middle-Aged Brain*. New York: Viking, 2010.

Ueland, Brenda. *If You Want to Write: A Book about Art, Independence and Spirit*. Floyd, VA: Sublime Books, 2014.

Vanderkam, Laura. *Off the Clock: Feel Less Busy While Getting More Done*. New York: Portfolio/Penguin, 2018.

Vernon, Mark. *The Philosophy of Friendship*. London: Palgrave Macmillan, 2005.

Wiking, Meik. *The Little Book of Hygge: Danish Secrets to Happy Living*. New York: William Morrow, 2017.

Zomorodi, Manoush. *Bored and Brilliant: How Spacing Out Can Unlock Your Most Productive and Creative Self*. New York: St. Martin's Press, 2017.

Articles

Allen, Summer. 2018. "The Science of Generosity." The Greater Good Science Center. https://ggsc.berkeley.edu/images/uploads/GGSC-JTF_White_Paper-Generosity-FINAL.pdf.

Amin, Amit. "The 31 Benefits of Gratitude You Didn't Know About: How Gratitude Can Change Your Life." Mind Content blog, June 2015. http://mymindcontentblog.blogspot.com/2015/06/the-31-benefits-of-gratitude-you-didnt.html.

Andreasen, Nancy C. "Secrets of the Creative Brain." *The Atlantic*, July/August 2014. https://www.theatlantic.com/magazine/archive/2014/07/secrets-of-the-creative-brain/372299.

Bahrampour, Tara. "Creativity Can Last Well into Old Age, as Long as Creators Stay Open to New Ideas." *The Washington Post*, November 21, 2013. https://www.washingtonpost.com/local/creativity-can-last-well-into-old-age-as-long-as-creators-stay-open-to-new-ideas/2013/11/21/31487172-52ca-11e3-a7f0-b790929232e1_story.html.

Barker, Eric. "How to Make Friends Easily and Strengthen the Friendships You Have." Time.com, March 14, 2014. http://time.com/24122/how-to-make-friends-easily-and-strengthen-the-friendships-you-have.

Berman, Marc G., John Jonides, and Stephen Kaplan. 2008. "The Cognitive Benefits of Interacting with Nature." *Psychological Science* 19, no. 12. https://pdfs.semanticscholar.org/5cef/86418e03740fc1a77eff6ba0b10541a2e223.pdf.

Brody, Jane E. "Using the Arts to Promote Healthy Aging." *The New York Times*, March 7, 2016. https://well.blogs.nytimes.com/2016/03/07/using-the-arts-to-promote-healthy-aging.

Bronson, Po, and Ashley Merryman. "The Creativity Crisis." *Newsweek*, July 10, 2010. http://www.newsweek.com/creativity-crisis-74665.

Carter, Sherrie Bourg. "Why Mess Causes Stress: 8 Reasons, 8 Remedies." PsychologyToday.com, March 14, 2012. https://www.psychologytoday.com/blog/high-octane-women/201203/why-mess-causes-stress-8-reasons-8-remedies.

Cohen, Gene D. "The Creativity and Aging Study: The Impact of Professionally Conducted Cultural Programs on Older Adults." April 30, 2006. https://www.arts.gov/sites/default/files/CnA-Rep4-30-06.pdf.

Collingwood, Jane. "The Importance of Friendship." PsychCentral.com, March 18, 2019. https://psychcentral.com/lib/the-importance-of-friendship.

Csikszentmihalyi, Mihaly. "The Pursuit of Happiness: Bringing the Science of Happiness to Life." http://www.pursuit-of-happiness.org/history-of-happiness/mihaly-csikszentmihalyi.

Dixit, Jay. "The Art of Now: Six Steps to Living in the Moment." PsychologyToday.com, November 1, 2008. https://www.psychologytoday.com/articles/200811/the-art-now-six-steps-living-in-the-moment.

Dixon, Alex. "Kindness Makes You Happy . . . and Happiness Makes You Kind." *Greater Good Magazine*, September 6, 2011. https://greatergood.berkeley.edu/article/item/kindness_makes_you_happy_and_happiness_makes_you_kind/.

Donnelly, Daniel A., and Edward J. Murray. 1991. "Cognitive and Emotional Changes in Written Essays and Therapy Interviews." *Journal of Social and Clinical Psychology* 10, no. 3: 334–50. https://guilfordjournals.com/

doi/10.1521/jscp.1991.10.3.334.

Dunbar, Robin. "How Many 'Friends' Can You Really Have?" *IEEE Spectrum*, May 31, 2011. https://spectrum.ieee.org/telecom/internet/how-many-friends-can-you-really-have.

Eaton, Judy, and Christine Tieber. 2017. "The Effects of Coloring on Anxiety, Mood, and Perseverance." *Art Therapy: Journal of the American Art Therapy Association* 34, no. 1. https://www.tandfonline.com/doi/abs/10.1080/07421656.2016.1277113.

Emmons, Robert. "Why Gratitude Is Good." *Greater Good Magazine*, November 16, 2010. https://greatergood.berkeley.edu/article/item/why_gratitude_is_good.

Emmons, Robert A., and Michael E. McCullough. "Counting Blessings Versus Burdens: An Experimental Investigation of Gratitude and Subjective Well-Being in Daily Life." *Journal of Personality and Social Psychology* 84, no. 2, 377–89. https://greatergood.berkeley.edu/images/application_uploads/Emmons-CountingBlessings.pdf.

Feist, Gregory J., and Mark A. Runco. 1993. "Trends in the creativity literature: An analysis of research in the *Journal of Creative Behavior* (1967–1989)." *Creativity Research Journal* 6, no. 3, 271–86. https://www.tandfonline.com/doi/abs/10.1080/10400419309534483.

Felps, Paula. "The Real Meditation Is Every Moment." LiveHappy.com, December 15, 2016. https://www.livehappy.com/practice/real-meditation-every-moment.

Fifield, Kathleen. "Give Yourself the Gift of a Good Life: Advice from Harvard's Top Happiness Researcher." *AARP The Magazine*, November 2018. https://www.aarp.org/health/healthy-living/info-2017/marriage-relationships-stress-happiness.html.

Frame, Selby. "Julianne Holt-Lunstad Probes Loneliness, Social Connection." American Psychological Association, October 18, 2017. https://www.apa.org/members/content/holt-lunstad-loneliness-social-connections.

Geoghegan, Tom. "What's the Ideal Number of Friends?" *BBC News Magazine*, March 3, 2009. http://news.bbc.co.uk/2/hi/7920434.stm.

Harrison, Kate L. "How Gratitude Can Make You More Creative and Innovative." Inc.com, November 16, 2016. https://www.inc.com/kate-l-harrison/how-gratitude-can-make-you-more-creative-and-innovative.html.

Horrigan, John B. "Lifelong Learning and Technology." Pew Research Center, March 2013. https://www.pewresearch.org/wp-content/uploads/sites/9/2016/03/PI_2016.03.22_Educational-Ecosystems_FINAL.pdf.

"In Praise of Gratitude." Harvard Health Publishing, November 2011. https://www.health.harvard.edu/mind-and-mood/in-praise-of-gratitude.

Ishizu, Tomohiro, and Semir Zeki. 2011. "Toward a Brain-Based Theory of Beauty." *PLoS ONE* 6, no 7: e21852. https://journals.plos.org/plosone/article?id=10.1371/journal.pone.0021852.

Karbo, Karen. "Friendship: The Laws of Attraction." PsychologyToday.com, November 1, 2006. https://www.psychologytoday.com/articles/200611/friendship-the-laws-attraction.

Kraft, Sheryl, and Irene Levine. "The Family Circle Survey: Girlfriends." *Family Circle.* https://www.familycircle.com/family-fun/relationships/the-family-circle-survey-girlfriends.

Leadem, Rose. "Even the Smallest Acts of Generosity Make You Happier, New Study Reveals." Entrepeneur.com, July 14, 2017. https://www.entrepreneur.com/article/297287.

Leong, Lai Yin Carmen, Ronald Fischer, and John McClure. 2014. "Are Nature Lovers More Innovative? The Relationship between Connectedness with Nature and Cognitive Styles." *Journal of Environmental Psychology* 40: 57–63. https://www.sciencedirect.com/science/article/pii/S0272494414000267.

MacVean, Mary. "For Many People, Gathering Possessions Is Just the Stuff of Life." *Los Angeles Times*, March 21, 2014. http://articles.latimes.com/2014/mar/21/health/la-he-keeping-stuff-20140322.

McMillan, Rebecca L., Scott Barry Kaufman, and Jerome Singer. 2013. "Ode to Positive Constructive Daydreaming." *Frontiers in Psychology* 4, article 626. https://www.ncbi.nlm.nih.gov/pmc/articles/PMC3779797/pdf/fpsyg-04-00626.pdf.

Morin, Amy. "7 Scientifically Proven Benefits of Gratitude." PsychologyToday.com, April 3, 2015. https://www.psychologytoday.com/blog/what-mentally-strong-people-dont-do/201504/7-scientifically-proven-benefits-gratitude.

Oppezzo, Marily, and Daniel L. Schwartz. 2014. "Give Your Ideas Some Legs: The Positive Effect of Walking on Creative Thinking." *Journal of Experimental Psychology: Learning, Memory, and Cognition* 40, no. 4: 1142–52. http://www.apa.org/pubs/journals/releases/xlm-a0036577.pdf.

Park, Soyoung Q., Thorsten Kahnt, Azade Dogan, Sabrina Strang, Ernst Fehr, and Philippe N. Tobler. 2017. "A Neural Link between Generosity and Happiness." *Nature Communications* 8, Article 15964. https://www.nature.com/articles/ncomms15964.

Parker-Pope, Tara. "The Talents of a Middle-Aged Brain." *The New York Times*, April 30, 2010. https://well.blogs.nytimes.com/2010/04/30/the-talents-of-a-middle-aged-brain.

Parry, Wynne. "How Gratitude Can Improve Your Life." LiveScience.com, January 1, 2013. https://www.livescience.com/25901-how-gratitude-improves-happiness.html.

Pavitt, Neil. "5 Brain Training Tips to Boost Creativity and Turn Ideas into Action." Chartered Management Institute, April 21, 2016. http://www.managers.org.uk/insights/news/2016/april/5-brain-training-tips-to-boost-creativity-and-turn-ideas-into-action.

Phillips, Melissa Lee. "The Mind at Midlife." American Psychological Association, April 2011. https://www.apa.org/monitor/2011/04/mind-midlife.

Roberts, Rosebud O., Ruth H. Cha, Michelle M. Mielke, Yonas E. Geda, Bradley F. Boeve, Mary M. Machulda, David S. Knopman, and Ronald C. Petersen. 2015. "Risk and Protective Factors for Cognitive Impairment in Persons Aged 85 and Older." *Neurology* 84, no. 18. http://n.neurology.org/content/84/18/1854.

Rothschild, Bianca. "How Mindful Meditation Boosts Creativity and Innovation." *The Huffington Post*, July 25, 2014. https://www.huffingtonpost.com/bianca-rothschild/the-science-of-how-medita_b_5579901.

Rudd, Melanie, Jennifer Aaker, and Michael Norton. 2013. "Leave Them Smiling: How Concretely Framing a Prosocial Goal Creates More Happiness." *NA—Advances in Consumer Research* 41. http://www.acrwebsite.org/volumes/1014720/volumes/v41/NA-41.

Schaie, K. Warner, and Sherry L. Willis. 2010. "The Seattle Longitudinal Study of Adult Cognitive Development." *ISSBD Bulletin* 57, no. 1: 24–9. https://www.ncbi.nlm.nih.gov/pmc/articles/PMC3607395/pdf/nihms446384.pdf.

"State of Create Study: Global Benchmark Study on AttLtudes and Beliefs about Creativity at Work, School and Home." Adobe, April 2012. https://www.adobe.com/aboutadobe/pressroom/pdfs/Adobe_State_of_Create_Global_Benchmark_Study.pdf.

Stuckey, Heather L., and Jeremy Nobel. 2010. "The Connection Between Art, Healing, and Public Health: A Review of Current Literature." *American Journal of Public Health* 100, no. 2: 254–63. https://www.ncbi.nlm.nih.gov/pmc/articles/PMC2804629/pdf/254.pdf.

Sulack, Pete. "How to Combat Stress with Gratitude." DailyPostive.com, January 19, 2016. https://www.thedailypositive.com/how-to-combat-stress-with-gratitude.

Turak, August. "Can Creativity Be Taught?" Forbes.com, May 22, 2011. https://www.forbes.com/sites/augustturak/2011/05/22/can-creativity-be-taught/#2122d21b1abb.

Walton, Mark S. "Why We're Hardwired for Midlife Reinvention." Nextavenue.com, November 19, 2012. https://www.nextavenue.org/why-were-hardwired-midlife-reinvention-and-boundless-potential.

Wislow, Eva. "18 Unusual Habits of Extremely Creative People." Jeffbullas.com. http://www.jeffbullas.com/18-unusual-habits-extremely-creative-people.

Wood, Alikay. "Soul Friends: Are Some People Inextricably Linked?" *Mysterious Ways*, February/March 2018: 33–5. https://www.guideposts.org/inspiration/miracles/soul-friends-are-some-people-inexplicably-linked.

Blogs, Websites, and Other Resources

Austin Kleon "is a writer and artist living in Austin, Texas." He is the *New York Times* best-selling author of the books *Steal Like an Artist, Show Your Work!,* and *Newspaper Blackout.* On his blog, he writes about creativity, art, and sometimes his personal life. https://austinkleon.com

Joshua Becker is the founder and editor of **Becoming Minimalist**, a website that inspires one million readers each month to own less and live more. He is also the best-selling author of the books *The More of Less* and *The Minimalist Home.* https://www.becomingminimalist.com

The mission of **Butterfly Coins** is to encourage and track random acts of kindness with beautiful solid brass trackable butterfly coins to be left behind with an act of kindness. Stories of the coins can be added to their website. https://butterflycoins.org

Creative Something is the place for discovering ideas and insights about your creativity. Tanner Christensen shares insights and ideas covering everything from art and psychology to the neuroscience of creative thinking. https://creativesomething.net

The Creativity Post: quality content on creativity, innovation, and imagination. http://www.creativitypost.com

"Dialoguing with Nature" workshop: Sue Schuerman pbragg@cfu.net

FundsforWriters: Tips and Tools for Serious Writers: online resource for writers; founded by C. Hope Clark in 2000; chosen as one of the 101 Best Writing Websites by *Writer's Digest* for the last 18 years in a row. https://fundsforwriters.com

KindSpring: Small Acts That Change the World, a Global Movement of Kindness: https://kindspring.servicespace.org

Live Happy magazine is dedicated to promoting and sharing authentic happiness, inspiring people to live purpose-filled, healthy, meaningful lives. https://www.livehappy.com

Magnolia Journal: quarterly lifestyle publication. https://magnolia.com/journal

Mary Jane's Farm: magazine, books, online sisterhood of "farmgirls". http://www.maryjanesfarm.org

Mindfulness: Finding Peace in a Frantic World: Dr. Danny Penman's website. http://franticworld.com

Random Acts of Kindness Foundation: https://www.randomactsofkindness.org/

Simplify Magazine: quarterly digital publication for families. https://simplifymagazine.com

Thirty Handmade Days:: Mique Provost's blog, author of *Make & Share Random Acts of Kindness*

World Gratitude Map: https://gratitude.crowdmap.com

Recommended Reading

The Artistic Mother: A Practical Guide to Fitting Creativity into Your Life by Shona Cole

Be a Blessing: A Journal for Cultivating Kindness, Joy, and Inspiration by Debbie Macomber

Be the Miracle: 50 Lessons for Making the Impossible Possible by Regina Brett

The Call of Solitude: Alonetime in a World of Attachment by Esther Buchholz

Chasing Slow: Courage to Journey Off the Beaten Path by Erin Loechner

Conscious Creativity: Look, Connect, Create by Philippa Stanton

Creative Is a Verb: If You're Alive, You're Creative by Patti Digh

Creativity Takes Courage: Dare to Think Differently by Irene Smit, Astrid van der Hulst, and the editors of *Flow* magazine

Discovering Joy in Your Creativity: You Are Made in the Image of a Creative God by Margaret Feinberg

Fiercehearted: Live Fully, Love Bravely by Holley Gerth

Gently Awakened: The Influence of Faith on Your Artistic Journey by Sara Joseph

Gratitude: Affirming One Another through Stories by Len Froyen

Happiness in this Life: A Passionate Meditation on Earthly Existence by Pope Francis

Happy by Design: How to Create a Home That Boosts Your Health & Happiness by Victoria Harrison

The I Hate to Housekeep Book: When and How to Keep House without Losing Your Mind by Peg Bracken

It's Never Too Late to Begin Again: Discovering Creativity and Meaning in Midlife and Beyond by Julia Cameron and Emma Lively

Keep Going: 10 Ways to Stay Creative in Good Times and Bad by Austin Kleon

Life is a Verb: 37 Days to Wake Up, Be Mindful, and Live Intentionally by Patti Digh

The Literary Ladies' Guide to the Writing Life: Inspiration and Advice from Celebrated Women Authors Who Paved the Way by Nava Atlas

Live Happy: Ten Practices for Choosing Joy by Deborah K. Heisz

Living Artfully: A Heart-full Guide of Ideas and Inspirations That Celebrate Life, Love, and Moments That Matter by Sandra Magsamen

Make & Share Random Acts of Kindness: Simple Crafts and Recipes to Give and Spread Joy by Mique Provost

Making Sense When Life Doesn't: The Secrets of Thriving in Tough Times by Cecil Murphey

Mary & Me: A Lasting Link Through Ink by Mary Potter Kenyon and Mary Jedlicka Humston

My Fringe Hours: Discovering a More Creative and Fulfilled Life by Jessica N. Turner

One Perfect Word: One Word Can Make All the Difference by Debbie Macomber

One Simple Act: Discovering the Power of Generosity by Debbie Macomber

One to One: Self-Understanding through Journal Writing by Christina Baldwin

Opening Up by Writing It Down: How Expressive Writing Improves Health and Eases Emotional Pain by James W. Pennebaker and Joshua M. Smyth

Real Artists Don't Starve: Timeless Strategies for Thriving in the New Creative Age by Jeff Goins

Refined by Fire: A Journey of Grief and Grace by Mary Potter Kenyon

Savor: Living Abundantly Where You Are, As You Are by Shauna Niequist

The Secret Life of the Grown-Up Brain: The Surprising Talents of the Middle-Aged Mind by Barbara Strauch

The Shy Writer: An Introvert's Guide to Writing Success by C. Hope Clark

Sidetracked Home Executives: From Pigpen to Paradise by Pam Young and Peggy Jones

Simple Abundance: A Daybook of Comfort and Joy by Sarah Ban Breathnach

Simplify Your Life: 100 Ways to Slow Down and Enjoy the Things That Really Matter by Elaine St. James

The Story You Need to Tell: Writing to Heal from Trauma, Illness, or Loss by Sandra Marinella

Taking Flight: Inspiration and Techniques to Give Your Creative Spirit Wings by Kelly Rae Roberts

Vital Friends: The People You Can't Afford to Live Without by Tom Rath

What Happy People Know: How the New Science of Happiness Can Change Your Life for the Better by Dan Baker and Cameron Stauth

World Enough & Time: On Creativity and Slowing Down by Christian McEwen

"Don't ask what the world needs. Ask what makes you come alive, and go do it. Because what the world needs is people who have come alive."

—HOWARD THURMAN

ACKNOWLEDGMENTS

"A book comes and says, 'Write me.' My job is to try to serve it to the best of my ability, which is never good enough, but all I can do is listen to it, do what it tells me and collaborate." —Madeleine L'Engle

The idea for this book stemmed from my mother's legacy of creativity and faith, and the words she left behind that led me to take my chosen craft of writing seriously while encouraging others to discover their own talents.

Then there was Michele Robbins. In 2012, an essay of mine on creativity was included in an anthology produced by the Familius publishing company run by her husband, Christopher. Michele called me on the phone, intrigued by what I'd written. "Do you have a book in you on this topic?" she'd asked. "I don't know. I might," I answered, thinking of the file folder on my desk labeled Creativity. "But right now, I'm trying to sell a book on couponing."

My mother had planted the seed. Michele had watered it. The blooming would come five years and four books after Familius published *Coupon Crazy: The Science, the Savings, and the Stories Behind America's Extreme Obsession.*

There were others who helped bring this book to fruition, most notably the husband who had been my biggest supporter and the eight children who were raised by a mom who often lived inside her head, lost in the flow of creating. Like my mother before me, one of my greatest desires is that each of them discovers their passion that will allow them to do the same. Then there were the Creative Sparks I profiled within these pages. Each spark was chosen to fit a chapter's theme, but even before I picked up a pen to begin writing, I knew my nephew Steve and brother Bill would be included. The others were revealed to me as writing progressed and the focus of each chapter solidified. That my final profile would be an artist who would help me create a mixed media project related to this book's topic was divine providence.

When I prayed for the perfect editor for this project, I was not prepared for the talent of Shaelyn Topolovec, who surprised me with her uncanny ability to hone in on each and every paragraph or idea I was not quite satisfied with in my first draft of the submitted manuscript.

I would be remiss not to thank my mentors, Shelly Beach and Cecil Murphey, as well as my initial lifelong learners group, many friends and family members who encouraged me in the writing of this book, especially David and Joan Kramer, who have consistently encouraged and supported me as a writer and speaker.

"We rise by lifting others."

—ROBERT INGERSOLL

ABOUT THE AUTHOR

Mary Potter Kenyon lives a creative life in Dubuque, Iowa, where she works as Program Coordinator for the Shalom Spirituality Center. A graduate of the University of Northern Iowa and a certified grief counselor, Mary is a popular public speaker for churches and women's groups and a workshop presenter and instructor for community colleges, libraries, and writers' conferences. She is widely published in newspapers, magazines, and anthologies, including ten *Chicken Soup for the Soul* books. Mary is the author of five previous Familius titles, including the award-winning *Refined by Fire: A Journey of Grief and Grace*. Visit her website at marypotterkenyon.com.

ABOUT FAMILIUS

Visit Our Website: www.familius.com
Familius is a global trade publishing company that publishes books and other content to help families be happy. We believe that the family is the fundamental unit of society and that happy families are the foundation of a happy life. We recognize that every family looks different, and we passionately believe in helping all families find greater joy. To that end, we publish books for children and adults that invite families to live the Familius Nine Habits of Happy Family Life: *love together, play together, learn together, work together, talk together, heal together, read together, eat together,* and *laugh together.* Founded in 2012, Familius is located in Sanger, California.

Connect
Facebook: www.facebook.com/paterfamilius
Twitter: @familiustalk, @paterfamilius1
Pinterest: www.pinterest.com/familius
Instagram: @familiustalk

FAMILIUS

The most important work you ever do will be within the walls of your own home.